T[illegible]

in[illegible]

You[illegible]

strong[illegible]

woman!!

Love,

Mienda

October 2014

TELL SOMEONE YOUR STORY

by Jean Belz

Contents

Foreword

JEAN FRANZENBURG BELZ was born in 1919 in Dolliver, Iowa. Her father, Paul Franzenburg, was a German immigrant who had earlier married a widowed mother of three — Bertha Watkins. To Paul and Bertha were born five more children: Paul Jr., Jean, Ruth, Wilhemina, and Collyn.

Paul Franzenburg Sr. was a butcher and meat retailer. The coming of the Great Depression meant that Jean and her siblings moved from small midwest town to small midwest town. Their 1934 arrival in Conrad, however, right at the center of Iowa, signaled the end of that nomadic life and the establishment at last of a sound business that continued for the next generation.

More significantly, the move to Conrad brought about the providential intersection between Jean's life as a young high school junior with that of Max Belz, a third generation grain, lumber, and coal dealer whose parents were mainstays in Conrad. Max was a recent Conrad High School grad employed by his uncle's daily newspaper in Brainerd, Minnesota. Even after relocating to Excelsior Springs, Missouri, though, and starting journalism studies at the University of Missouri, Max found his heart tugged toward Conrad — partly to join his father in business but perhaps mostly to pursue an even more passionate love.

After her own graduation in 1936, Jean left for Hamline University in Minnesota. But the very next year, it was back to Conrad — and an October wedding in an unseasonal snowstorm. The bride was only 18.

Two years later — but only after the untimely death of Jean's own mother — the young couple's own family of eight children began to arrive. Julie (Al Lutz), Joel (Carol), Mark (Linda), Mary (Steve Kaufmann), Tim (Sharon), Nathaniel (Mindy), Andrew (Mary Anna), and Sara (Jim Drexler), along with 31 grandchildren and 31 more great-grandchildren, all survived her at her death.

Fully as significant as her biological family, though, was the work God did in Jean's heart (along with that of her husband Max) during the 1940s. Their business prospered — but the gospel of Jesus Christ in God's Word prospered even more, prompting them to leave everything they had in 1946 to invest themselves in the work of the church and, ultimately, Christian education. Through the Bible Presbyterian Church at Cono and Cono Christian School, thousands of lives were profoundly shaped over the next 64 years.

It was for only half that extended tenure, though, that Max and Jean Belz were allowed to labor together; he died in 1978. For 32 more years, from the center of Cono's campus, her role as mother, teacher, essayist and perceptive reader, correspondent, wise friend, godly counselor, homemaker, gardener, musician and sports fan continued until her death only slightly diminished.

Through all her 91 years, Jean Belz's frugality — with money, possessions, time, and words — equipped and enabled her to be generous with others. She knew from experience that salvation is not something to be earned, but a gift from God. And she lived her whole long life passing God's good gifts on to those around her.

Jean wrote a regular column for Cono's newsletter, the *Cono Bulletin*. These columns form this collection of her writings, which she started in 1990 and continued to within two weeks of her death in September, 2010.

The Beautiful Woman

for Grandma Belz: "Stay by the stuff."

Having lived all of one's life in the plains among corn,
Wife of one, mother of eight, a multitude's grandmother;
Having loved more than a thousand young people
By teaching them Latin and English, praying with them,
Housing and hugging them, barking orders at them;
Having set thousands of tables and boiled as many pots
Of coffee and perhaps ten thousand eggs;
Having washed and folded, ironed and organized,
Stitched and darned, written essays about such things,
Read countless novels, books of poetry, different Bibles,
Sent letters, cards, checks, left encouraging notes;
Having turned soil every year for decades with those
Who had no idea how to garden, having explained how
To not only garden but hang wash on a line;
Having spent one's youth faithfully supporting
A zealous preacher who had his own issues, seriously,
But loved the Lord with his heart, who died
An untimely and painful death by prostate cancer;
Having become old among all of one's possessions;

Having lately also endured the deaths of Billie, Paul, Rudy,
With more to come—the story of loss is still being written;
To stand, now, in the kitchen preparing food for family
That straggles in at all hours on the night before Thanksgiving
In a homemade house that creaks in a freezing wind:
That just doesn't sound like a lot of fun to me.
To go right on working, to keep reminding oneself of heaven,
To endure disappointment, failure, sinfulness, death,
Bills, prodigal children, prodigal grandchildren,
Prodigal students, prodigal siblings, and a prodigal self;
To resist fleeing to a place less inclement,
Because that's what I want to do, to jet off,
To surround myself with beautiful, self-contained people,
To listen to music and attend plays, to float,
To become lost in the lights of this visible world
Instead of giving myself to its grim little gears,
Sacrificing myself for its orphans and scoundrels,
Staying by the stuff, as someone once wrote;
Doing all this and not even being able to take credit,
Not even really wanting to talk much about it,
In fact, counting it joy: All this and heaven too.
Lord, let my mind be so much of this world
And my heart be at home somewhere beyond it.

—Aaron Belz

Jean Franzenburg (left) with sister Wilhelmina (Billy) in 1937

Tell someone your story

July-August 1990

We were gathered at a bridal shower a few nights ago, and I watched the honoree open a box containing a set of towels — white with rose stripes and so inviting. My mind went back over 53 years. I wanted to tell the bride-to-be a story about my wedding, but this wasn't the time. Silently, I recalled that in 1937 as the Depression years were easing a bit and I was preparing to be married, I was doing housework for an older friend for ten cents an hour. (These earnings bought my trousseau!) One day my friend came home from shopping with a lovely yellow towel set for me — to begin housekeeping. How beautiful can a towel be! How happy can a girl be! Is there anyone who wants to know?

Well, my eighteen-year-old grandson wanted to know, just a few weeks ago. This was the time to tell my story and many others. As he and I were driving a long distance together, somehow memories of more than half a century crowded in and spilled out as fast as I could talk. Courtship, marriage, hard times, good times, births, deaths, homes, churches, and most important, decisions and philosophies of his forebears. He was rapt, and I was rapt. "Why haven't I heard this before?" he demanded.

It takes energy and time and courage to bring the past up to the present, but we need to get things in focus for the sake of the health and balance of our children and grandchildren. Find a listener. Tell your story.

> *"And it shall be when thy son asketh thee in time to come, saying, What is this? that thou shalt say unto him, By strength of hand the Lord brought us out from Egypt, from the house of bondage."*
>
> — Exodus 13:14

Manners matter

August-September 1990

What is your rule?

Several months ago our pastor declared that the key to a good marriage is courtesy. It appealed to me as a strong, good statement, and I stored it away in my thinking. Not two weeks ago he said it again! He really thinks so! So it is not just an idea worth remembering, but it is something to go by.

How can courtesy be established? It's said that in the Jonathan Edwards household, courtesy was the rule. What better lineage to emulate! But you say, "How stuffy. Aren't we all in this together? We love and understand each other. Why stand on ceremony?" Do you sometimes ask the Lord to take away self-seeking? Perhaps He wants you to begin with manners. Each of the Ten Commandments calls for selflessness before God or for considering the other person first.

Does a tap on the door before entering a study or a bedroom indicate a lack of intimacy or real love? Of course not. It is a sign of respect and thoughtfulness that honors rather than presumes. Does refraining from opening a letter addressed to a spouse show lack of interest or trust? On the contrary, it is a habit that builds credibility and love. What about oafish behavior? Since the oaf's heart is big, won't he be understood? And insults. Aren't they friendly? Not really. Kindness helps.

I once asked the son of a woman newly in charge of meal preparations what we could do to help. He said, "I think all mom needs is a little appreciation." Who does not? What husband or wife does not? To appreciate is to cherish. To cherish is to hold dear and protect.

By His Grace

June 1979

Is there a way out of frustration and discouragement? I know there is. I have lived in this community for thirty years. My husband and I came here in the late forties — we had four children. In the years following, four more children were born. They are grown now and my husband has gone on to heaven. But I want to tell you what has made these thirty years full to the brim of love, comfort, excitement, and satisfaction even in disappointment and sorrow.

I was born in 1919 to a "Yankee" mother and a German immigrant father. There were eight children, three older and five of us younger. In the midst of music, books, sports, good times, bad times, school and church I learned to scorn the Scriptures and the Lord Jesus Christ. This may seem unlikely, but as I look back now I realize how easily a child's ideas are molded. One day when I was quite young I asked my mother about heaven. The question was often on my mind. Instead of answering for herself she said, "Daddy doesn't think there is a heaven or hell." Later, in a liberal college, when I was trying to work a required Bible course into my schedule, my adviser dismissed the problem and said parts of the Bible were not worth reading.

At the same time I learned from my parents a great sense of values: contentment without "things," the importance of hard work, frugality, and the sanctity and joy of a marriage and home. My husband and I were married in October, 1937. The years following were busy, profitable ones. We tried to maintain strict discipline with our children, integrity in business, hospitality in our home, and faithfulness in church attendance and tithing. This was all rewarding—but it was not enough. I felt a gnawing dissatisfaction. I worked hard to keep a clean record of behavior but I failed. I lost my temper, was late for appointments, tangled with friends, and was impatient with my husband and children. But my pride was unreasonable. I only tried harder and refused to admit my faults.

One day in 1943 I overheard a minister friend ask the man he was conversing with this question: "What is sin?" I scarcely heard the rest of their conversation. The Lord used those works to make me see myself — examine myself. I was sinful, absolutely unable to have a clear record no matter how upright I may have appeared. I needed help, a way out. The Lord did not let me rest until I confessed my need of Him and laid my sins on Jesus. I rested then on Scripture after Scripture — Ephesians 2:8 and 9, 1 John 5:13, Isaiah 43:11 — hundreds of passages. The Bible is true!

I understood what personal peace is, what a home devoted to the Lord Jesus Christ is, and what fellowship in a church with like-minded Christians is. After that day my life was new—the grass was greener, the sky was bluer, my husband and children were dearer. I walked into the garden or drove down the road and knew that all the colors, shapes, and textures before me were made by the hand of the living God. I recall looking into the face of one of my sons as he was singing in a Christmas program. I could see reality and hope. My whole reason for being was changed. I had purpose, loving and miraculous, in Christ.

A few years later the Lord guided us out of the business world into preaching and teaching. He brought us here and cared for us in marvelous ways. I praise Him for His goodness — joy in this life and hope of heaven for my family — extending even to my father who became warm and sensitive to the Scriptures as he grew older.

Do you know this Savior, the Lord Jesus Christ, who can make you and all things new and full of meaning?

When the worldling, sick at heart,
Lifts his soul above;
When the prodigal looks back
To his father's love;
When the proud man, in his pride,
Stoops to seek thy face;
When the burdened brings his guilt
To thy Throne of grace;
Hear then in love, Oh Lord, the cry
In heav'n, thy dwelling place on high.

—Horatius Bonar

COURAGE—*June 7, 1948, was a watershed day for the Belz family and their ministry at Cono. For two years, God had blessed the little rural church, bringing new families and new Biblical awareness to everyone involved. But then, a refusal by the Cono leadership to follow the liberal program of the mainline Presbyterian denomination led to a legal order by the denomination forbidding the congregation from meeting in the attractive church building*

they had just extensively remodeled. Stunned, the officers and their families gathered that afternoon in a school yard just across the road to begin mapping their future. Here, Max Belz (center front) and elder LeRoy Gardner examine the eviction papers. Jean Belz (holding her daughter Mary) could scarcely have imagined how her opportunities for service and influence over the next 60 years would be multiplied.

Jean Belz

Worship in Spirit

October-November 1990

On a recent Sunday morning as the offering basket was passed during the worship hour, I felt a little shiver of excitement. For a moment I was puzzled. And then I realized that it was not an unfamiliar experience, but that whenever the offering is taken I feel a thrill of anticipation and privilege, whatever the size of my gift.

My thoughts hurried on to the hymns. With the announcement of each one, I enjoyed finding the page, raising my croaky voice in praise, and marveling that the author's Christian experience so nearly matched mine.

And to still another — as we are called to pray. I bow my head in submission and confidence before the Lord and know: "This can't be taken away. No one can rob me of the privilege of prayer."

It wasn't always so. As an unbelieving teenager, defying the truth of the scriptures, I was unaware of the depth and power of being in God's presence. But soon after becoming a believer, I heard a Bible conference speaker instruct his listeners in the act of worship. Forty-four years after that conference, my whole self still quickens and responds to his words: "Sing the hymn! Bow your head in prayer! Have your gift ready!" Add to this the reading and the preaching of God's word. It is health and safety to my soul.

Winter, 1990

December-January 1991

Dear Mark and Linda,

When you were insistent that I not drive home to Iowa from St. Louis on the snow and ice, I know you were concerned for my welfare — but I'm glad I was not deprived of the trip the next day when the sun came out after the storm.

Leaving St. Louis at noon, I enjoyed Missouri's bare winter beauty for miles and miles. The dark rivers, heavy timber, and cheerful sunlight were familiar and lovely. Above Hannibal I unwrapped my sandwich and ate it with relish, along with my favorite grape soda. I soon began to see small chunks of snow along the shoulder of the highway. They had dropped off south-bound trucks and cars and were a sure sign of snow ahead. For a moment it was forbidding, and I felt a little dread of the road over the Des Moines River. But the sunshine kept beckoning and seemed to propel me right over the bridge into Iowa.

Now it was three o'clock in the afternoon, a light sifting of snow covered everything — fields, ditches, fences, trees, gardens, shrubs. I was enveloped in beauty — a powdered sugar carpet lit with pale gold sunlight and capped with immense blue sky like a cerulean-lined bowl. (That word has tempted me for a long time, and this is surely the time to use it.)

I stopped on the side of the road above Mount Pleasant for a cookie, an apple, and coffee from my stores. My excitement grew. I couldn't take in all of the loveliness of the trees and hills. I wanted everyone I knew to see it too. But there was more. The thin covering became a thick layer of fresh white snow like heavy, shiny frosting on a cake, and along the ridge of every fence and ditch were snow dunes, glistening and perfectly shaped. Houses and farms had an enameled look as the snow continued to light them all, effortlessly and dazzling.

I looked and looked and knew the time was short. The sunlight turned more gold. Shadows darkened and ponds reflected dark silver with traces of pink. Suddenly great shafts of brilliant orange crossed and re-crossed each other high in the western sky. But near Iowa City the color faded, and I thought the spectacle was over. I looked again, and the same streaks had turned to deep pink — so beautiful, so brief. Even while I fixed it all in my mind, the vivid color became heavy and gray and dark against the lingering light on the horizon. All I needed was provided — time to think it all over — God's glory and a safe trip home.

Playground Art — The Best of Ballet

February 1991

A rush and a flutter drew my glance outside my dining room window. Eight or ten goldfinches had just exchanged perches on the feeder and the bare sumac branches. On this February day the gentleman finch wore a tarnished green coat nearly like his mate's — he won't don his vivid yellow and black until late spring.

Now they are quiet again, their sleek heads turning and poking into the feeder right in time to the Tchaikovsky I'm enjoying inside. Now and then a single finch performs alone, flitting to a new perch. He catches the bright eyes of his fellows, but there's no alarm. The others go on eating with rhythm and poise. Then at some signal the whole troupe change branches again. What marvelous direction!

But in the background is a bigger production. The lunch break brings the younger children to the tennis court to play. The scene sparkles in the late winter sunlight. Skate boards, roller skates, balls, and play wagons all go into action. The cues seem clear. Little boys with legs like iron run wildly around the edge of the court. A basketball swished through the hoop misses the runners nicely. I hold my breath as a skateboard star cuts through a band of little girls in pink, puffy jackets, their shiny blonde hair streaming from under pink caps. The girls are indifferent. Their skates are on and they glide easily — imperiously — around the court.

A few players are still in the wings. A skater stops to help her sister with a stubborn strap. A chubby boy tugs at a wagon upsetting two little girls and himself. But they are well padded and cheerfully push and pull to try again. One skater stoops and gently pulls a forlorn figure in a corner to her feet. She joins the cast, timid but happy. A little pixie with black eyes and hair darts like a quicksilver among the bold, strong boys. In lieu of wheels or ball, one small boy simply runs, stops short, and pirouettes exuberantly. Dashes, skids, stops, starts, bumps, and tumbles continue with ease. This choreography is open and free — no tension or pain. It is a spectacle in pink and pale gold. There's the bell. All over.

Satisfying sources

May-June 1991

Some of our most stimulating and encouraging ideas come to us from the experiences of others. These jewels give us help and comfort along the way and build the fabric of our lives.

As I was approaching middle age and thinking, rather fondly, that the years would bring easier times and fewer problems, I read Isabel Kuhn's *In the Arena.* She tells how, after years of serving the Lord in China, she became entangled in troubles of her own making — became a spectacle. Instead of a period of ease, it was one of chastening, but to her edification and to God's glory.

Edith Schaeffer writes about a young woman whose thinking process had been shattered by drugs before she arrived at L'Abri. She could not grasp the philosophy and doctrine being taught or discussed. But the Schaeffers found that she was able to absorb simple, wholesome reading, and she gradually came to the point of embracing biblical truths. Sometimes it helps to leave off or delay sophistication.

Catherine Marshall, quoting Elizabeth B. Dodds, devotes an entire chapter in *Something More* to the testimony of the family of Jonathan Edwards and to

God's faithfulness to his descendants. She tells us that, in a period of stress, Sarah Edwards went to her husband for help. He counseled her in much the same way a professional might nowadays, having her list the pressures surrounding her and then helping her to deal with them, one at a time. She regained her emotional strength.

Even Jane Austen, who may or may not have been a Christian, delights the reader as her heroine attempts to impress the man she so admires. "I have just learnt to love a hyacinth," says Catherine. "So," the gentleman replies quite coolly. "Who can tell? If you have learnt to love a hyacinth, you may, in time, come to love a rose."

Are you listening? Have you been reading? If you have learned to enjoy the gold mine that is found in the writings and lives of others, who knows? "Yourself" (as Joe Gargery says in Dickens's *Great Expectations*) may someday become a source.

Uneasy times, His times

July-August 1991

As a child, after anguishing amid hot tears and aching throat over the sufferings of Black Beauty and Ginger in Anna Sewell's well-known classic, I rejoiced over the final chapter. There Black Beauty tells the reader, "I have now been in this happy place a whole year." A whole year! What relief! Black Beauty is safe. If he can be all right for that long, surely nothing bad will happen again.

Growing up, I sometimes used a year of happiness or stability as a kind of guarantee of its continuing. Is time the great deliverer? I have never caught up with the years. Family, so dear to me, died — my mother, my father, my husband. My children were born. The childhood years that had seemed so long to me now flashed by as each boy or girl left the nest. Fifty-two years since we suffered such sorrow at the death of my mother. More than twelve years since my husband went on to heaven. My granddaughter was once told, rather lightly, that she could not touch a certain one hundred-year-old tea set until she was twenty-five. She was discouraged. By that time, the tea set would be one hundred and twenty-five years and more inaccessible than ever.

Are memories enough? Well, it takes a full-time

"year watcher" to keep the memories from telescoping, to keep them sorted out. What to do? I'd better make every effort to see and talk with the real, live subjects rather than indulge in too many picture albums or too much nostalgia. Catch the years of children between five and fifteen, so often neglected in the face of family pressures. And read. And write. Since years, even decades, and months, weeks, days, and hours melt away, the best answer comes from the Scriptures. I can redeem the time. My times are in His hands.

Divorce

September-October 1991

When I read a newspaper column, an essay, an opinion, I enjoy a light touch — some relief from the burden of the subject itself. Oh, it's important to follow the thread of serious intent of the writer, especially if I agree or if he says something I've been wishing I could express. I might even find myself forgiving other points of disagreement if he just says the "right thing" somewhere along the line.

Not so with the subject of divorce. From time to time we can read new findings from the experts on this matter. One year we hear that children are not affected nearly as much as we might think by the breaking up of the home. A year later we learn that the effects are adverse and far-reaching. Some time ago a lawyer told me about a fourteen-year-old girl whose parents he was seeking to help as they considered divorce. The daughter declared over and over, bravely and cheerfully, that everything would be all right if the marriage was broken. And suddenly she burst into a torrent of tears! It wasn't all right and never would be.

Whatever you can do to help preserve a home is important. Your interference will never be as hurtful as the breakup of the family. I wrote the following paragraphs at such a critical time. No reason given by a spouse, infidelity, boredom, indifference, is good enough.

". . . any thought of or move toward unfaithfulness must not be considered. If you have compromised your honor and integrity, then you must turn around, reverse your actions, and begin at once to re-establish your home and family — perhaps for the first time establish a relationship based on confidence and respect and love that you have never experienced before. You do not owe anyone else anything unless it is an apology or an admission of wrongdoing and a declaration of your intention to restore your marriage. This action will command respect from everyone involved. To pursue a course of deception and weakness means sordidness, cruelty and misery to everyone concerned.

"Don't think the course of action I've laid out is impossible. I have seen it taken. Afterwards the person wondered how he could ever have thought of breaking up his home and bringing this cruel treatment on his family. Anybody can take up with women or men who are not their wives or husbands. And if a woman is willing to take up with a man who is not her husband, she is not to be counted on. She is not true, and she is cruel, because she doesn't mind seeing others suffer. It takes somebody to remain faithful and to encourage and cheer a spouse and children. Of course, it takes effort. It does for everyone."

And you can be sure there is suffering where there is unfaithfulness no matter how good things may appear on the surface. Cherish your wife. Cherish your husband.

No light touch here except for the light touch of real love.

January again

November–December 1991

Just as I was ready to write about the glories of January, a five-day fog settled in — at least five days. But this doesn't scare me off. I know from years of experience that there are glories in January. Even on this dark day, there are six finches on the feeder and another fighting for position. Mr. Cardinal makes himself at home right in the middle of a makeshift feeder, his incredibly bright coat establishing his position. This is a sort of day that sends us to the sewing machine, to the furniture stripping, or to cleaning a closet as we put away Christmas decorations. Strip the halls of boughs of holly! Is it too dull? Then write letters — nothing is more appreciated or rewarding. Or, best of all, for you, read a book. That's bliss.

And the sun may come out. The days start lengthening on December 22, almost imperceptibly as we are in the throes of holiday excitement. We get back into the routine of jobs, school, midwinter responsibility. Then watch the sun move slowly north on the western horizon each evening. On a bright day, wherever you are, notice the slant of the January sun. It couldn't be directly overhead, or it would be June. Instead the sunshine comes through the window almost horizontally, lighting the room at a beautiful angle just when we need it most. If you take a drive, the artistry of the bare trees against the sky or the black creek outlined with white snow banks will be more than you can take in.

A seed catalog arrives, the houseplants push out buds, and as you sit in your cozy chair in the January sunlight, anticipation of a lovely garden closely approaches realization. Now the students are looking at new schedules. Seniors are thinking, "One more semester." Basketball tournaments beckon, and chorale concerts and tour loom. Adults are examining their finances and experiencing a sort of purge. It may be that the temperature will creep up to 45 or 50 degrees on one of these days, and, when you step outside, you will poke your boot into a puddle and sniff. What is that hint in the air? Shelley is both Scriptural and comforting. "If winter come, can spring be far behind?"

Jean Belz

Each one a singular creation

January-February 1992

"Just how many boys do you have?" an older lady asked me one day. I looked at the backs of three close-cropped heads visible over the top of the church pew and understood her confusion. Were they really so much alike? I love to remember the day two small boys paused halfway down the stairs, still sleepy from their naps, and I said to the first one, "Are you my sweet brown-eyed boy?" Before I could even things up, the second one asked, a little sadly, "What color are my eyes?"

Now that I am older, it is my turn to be confused. Three little brothers come to church, and I am embarrassed when I can't tell them apart, but their parents know which one is always hungry, who is stubborn, who is quiet, or who is wiggly, and they delight in these contrasts. When, in September, twenty-five or more boys file in for supper, their young faces, their slicked down hair, and their school shirts and trousers defy distinction, but in December we see their family resemblances and we recognize their every mood — anger, disappointment, loneliness, enthusiasm, exuberance, or satisfaction. There is no one else in the world just like me. There is no one else just like you.

In the excitement of getting acquainted with a new computer, my daughter consulted her computer-wise brothers — all older — on some fine points. Their responses were nearly as fascinating to her as the equipment itself. The oldest, across country, gave her some fatherly advice, generally good, but not specific. The second one, always kind, said he'd drop by in his lunch hour. And he did. The third issued several bullet-like instructions, sharp and accurate. The fourth, the expert of them all, used so many terms known only to experts that they were beyond her. And the fifth, some miles away, said, "Don't listen to any of them. I'll be there in two days."

Have you had someone say, "I can always pick out one of your family!"? I have, and I ask, "How can that be?" The response: "Oh, by his voice. Or his cheekbones. Or he looks like his father. Or like his uncle." What comfort that brings. What a sense of belonging. I wonder why we are so prone to give it up, to sell out so cheaply — daughters fearing that they will be like their mothers and sons like their fathers. Instead of blurring our heritage with our indifference or, worse, disdain, we should hold it in high regard, not out of pride but with grateful appreciation.

And the differences that lie within that heritage? Well, they make us who we are. They are treasures, and they make us rich. Don't forget the color of their eyes.

Jean Belz

"And how can they hear without a preacher?"

March-April 1992

Mr. Ted Noé said, some years ago, "Problems of the church should be settled from the pulpit." Just imagine sitting in the pew, hearing the Word of God expounded, and going away satisfied that all of your concerns were resolved. Too good to be true? Too far removed from reality? I'm sure it happens, but not often enough. Instead of having an expectant attitude, we are more apt to be surprised if the preaching and a solution to a problem coincide. What does it take for effective preaching?

Well, it takes a high view of the Scriptures. A high view? My German immigrant father, in the early part of the century, conveyed to me a high view of the news media, of the Senate, of the public school, and other such American institutions. But we have learned, bitterly, that all of these institutions are fallible. Not so the Scriptures. When the preacher takes the high ground, we in the pew are transported into the reality of God's truth.

And the preacher needs courage. He must believe that what he says at a particular time will be applied to the life of the listener by the Holy Spirit. Surely if he can be objective, he can preach more freely. In years past, I would frequently say to my preacher-husband, "But you didn't say this," or, "You should have added that," or, "People won't know for sure what you mean." And he would say, "But I can't say everything every time." And I learned to understand that. Have you ever heard a speaker try to take care of every eventuality as he goes along? Dull! He loses you.

As we sit in the pew, and we hear God's Word come close to our lives and hearts, we can make it all more and more complicated, consider being counseled further, resist simple obedience, or turn it off altogether. Or we can stop doing what we shouldn't be doing, begin to do what we should be doing, and submit to the Lord and to our fellow Christians.

When our pastor was preaching about the problems of the early church as related in Acts 15, he noted that James closed his instructions to the assembly by saying,

"For Moses has been preached in every city from the earliest times and is read in the synagogues on every Sabbath."

And the pastor added, "The Word of God is there. Let it do its work. Turn it loose."

Jean Belz

The incomparable gift of language

May-June 1992

Some time ago I dug up my courage and used the word *cerulean*. It was a pleasure and relief after years of wanting to. With that dubious success, I determined to inject a word of similar loveliness into a paragraph, i.e. *halcyon*: Inject! What am I saying? Just as I was making sure of the best usage, out came the news that the drug, Halcion, might be dangerous. I would say it took the starch out of me, but who of you knows what starch is? Where are the halcyon days?

Being a purist isn't easy. When youngsters read such words as *gay* or *faggot*, beautifully used in Sir Walter Scott's poetry, and grin self-consciously at each other, I take the opportunity to tell them these are good words and don't have to be given up — yet. A teacher suggested to me that it's all right to say, "It's him," and grammar rules are shifting at best. It's enough to bring on retirement.

But why quarrel when there are thousands of wonderful words that go almost unused? And they are not obscure words, arcane in their meaning. They are verbs with strong roots and vital prefixes, adjectives to replace the word *interesting*, and nouns to be used in place of *thing*. Even wee little words can take on astounding proportions. One of our sons complained, when he was very small, that the parents of a little friend allowed her to use words that were too big. "What kind of words?" We were curious. "Well," he answered, "when she prays, she says, 'Be with us *as* we go home, and you know *as* is a pretty big word.'" And it is. Think of it — "as I eat my supper" . . . "as I get well" . . . "as the years go by" . . . "as the centuries roll."

Why not read new words, learn new words, use new words? Urge them on your children at mealtime or on your grandchildren in a letter. Praise God for language, an incomparable gift from Him to us.

Jean Belz

Stewardship and the Good Life

July-August 1992

Not long ago a handsome brochure arrived in the mail from an investment firm. It was too inviting to put down. I could see from the sample pages pictured there of various kinds of accounts how I might have prospered through the years if I had invested even modest sums in the best way. Why didn't I do it?

Just look at this! I might have hundreds of thousands of dollars stowed away if I had just done it right! We were always frugal. And we were solvent. Where did we slip up?

Now I recall my husband's saying, "If it takes every cent we have, we must train these children for the Lord." But, of course, it wouldn't take all that, I thought. Things would surely get easier. But they didn't. It is a continuing struggle — and a wonderful struggle.

Does this mean that everyone who trains his child properly is destined to go without a bank account? Not at all. There are wiser, more capable men and women than we who know how to get dollars, keep them, and add to them. And these same folks help the rest of us in our endeavors. In America we are blessed with the freedom to earn and give.

Besides, we have only so much capacity to take in things whether we are rich or poor. R. G. LeTourneau, a business man for God, said he could eat only one meal at a time and sleep in only one bed at a time. My husband once said that we could eat asparagus roots, if necessary, to keep going. Why he equated asparagus roots with stringency, I'm not sure. Actually, through the years we enjoyed not only the luxury of asparagus along with other choice fresh foods, tasty meats, and delicious baked goods, but also the company of many of God's best servants at our table.

We all like to be on our own. I advise my children and grandchildren to save and invest for at least a degree of independence in later years. To be guaranteed all we need or want till we die sounds marvelous.

But there is no such man-made guarantee. Our best hope is obedience to the Scriptures.

Jean Belz

Stairstep wonder

September-October 1992

As children, we were privileged in our family to grow up without partiality from our parents or differences made because of age. At least, that's the way it seemed to me. To be sure, in a harried moment, our mother might say to us as ten- or twelve-year-olds, "You were less trouble when you were babies!" But I never assumed that she wanted us to be babies again. Our father often exclaimed about the wonder of a baby — the sweetness of the tiny foot or hand or cheek, and the delightful sound of the sigh as the nipple reached the eager lips. But he also displayed intense interest in our first piano lessons, he was compassionate when a romance took a bad turn, and he was ready with a loan (with interest) when his children or grandchildren ran short. I'm pretty sure, as a mother of eight, that I didn't consciously try to imitate Dad in all these areas, but when a doctor friend once kindly advised, "You can't meet the needs of all those youngsters (ages one to seventeen)," I thought, "Yes, I can."

Of course, I couldn't. But one need I could meet was appreciation for each child. Long ago, when a friend remarked, "You know four months is such a sweet little age," I didn't know, but I found out. Now think of all that happens to a child in his first two years. He walks, he talks, he feeds himself, he makes friends, he dances and sings, he freely names the name of God, he can even help set the table and put clean clothes away! If you want to see yourself, watch him. He isn't terrible. He is irresistible.

When he is four, he is a pre-schooler, and his mother had better hang onto him. Her days with him are numbered. How did he get to be so bright? He seems to know everything. Does he even need to go to school? Maybe not, for a while. He is bold one moment and dependent the next. He is delightful company on the way to the grocery store with his mother or to the lumber yard with his father. And he can listen for the baby to wake up from a nap. Oh, treasured days!

Are five to fifteen the forgotten years? I hope not. This is the time that strong bodies are developed and habits and interests are formed. We need to keep a close, cheerful watch as the whole world opens up to these youngsters. A grandson, after accompanying his father on a pastoral call, reported, "We went to see a lady whose husband died, and all her children grew up to be people." It happens. It would take volumes to list everything that can be learned in this ten-year period. It is crammed with "golden moments"... learning to read and comprehend, to dribble a ball, to bake cookies or scramble eggs, to drive a nail and mow a lawn, to "carry" in math, to play the piano or sing parts, to sew on a button or make a skirt, to baby-sit and drive a car, to do the laundry or pack a suitcase, to use bigger words, and to operate the computer. Suddenly, our daughters have become desirable young women, and, along with our sons, are being sought by friends, colleges, and employers. "It's too soon," we cry, but isn't it what we worked and planned for?

The college years are fleeting and, in some ways, artificial, not real. But this is the time jobs, careers, and spouses are chosen. Can we support these choices happily and positively without interfering? What a balance is needed! We may or may not see our dreams fulfilled in a youngster . . . but this isn't the important part. What riches we enjoy when our children and grandchildren receive us warmly into their homes, and we see that they are rising above the mediocre and are taking the high road of principles and spirituality. Don't lose a moment.

It's worth it to mind manners

November-December 1992

The matter of manners keeps rearing its head. All day long every day, it seems. But why press the matter? It must be because crudities, uncouth behavior, and lack of gratitude and appreciation are well-nigh intolerable. And the responsibility we have for the youngsters about us is awesome. If we don't remind them, who will? But if a reminder means a confrontation, is it worth it? Of course. Are we adults exemplary? Sometimes. Sometimes not. But we must aim to be. Even the way we consider all of these questions should be in a context of good manners.

How far do we go? A friend of mine, in musing over the fine line between suggestion and punishment, asked, "After all, do you punish a boy every time he doesn't break his bread in two?" I passed this story on to a group of students in an effort to impress on them the great wisdom needed by adults, but at least one boy missed the point and asked in wonderment, "Well, why would you want to break your bread in two!" Whereupon the others shouted, "Because it's good manners!" Rewards do creep in now and then.

A particular school boy was exclaiming loudly,

"When I first came [to school], I had no manners. When I wanted green beans, I reached all the way across the table for them." And he did — while his table companions (who had been at school all of three weeks longer) looked on incredulously.

Why shouldn't he reach across the table? (After all, we can be glad he eats green beans.) Or why shouldn't a girl use a spoon to eat mashed potatoes? And doesn't it save time to simply shout "Telephone!" at someone who's been called? If we are comfortable in smelly clothes with unkempt hair and our feet up, should anyone care? What makes manners important anyway?

Phyllis McGinley, in *Sixpence in Her Shoe*, says, "Manners are morals," and she explains that the respect we show one another almost invariably is an extension or an illustration of one of the Ten Commandments or of the summation of the law. Someone may say, "I'll take my friends or my children 'in the rough.' They seem to be more sincere that way." Is there a reason that good manners and sincerity can't go together? McGinley maintains that we can teach children certain physical responses before they learn to understand genuine kindness just as they learn simple facts of mathematics before they understand the theory. She says, "Manners are the exercise of the body for the sake of the mind and soul."

Who knows when the good behavior, the niceties,

will travel from the head to the heart? Order and courtesy and thoughtfulness are surely of the Lord. Let's not be robbed.

JEAN BELZ

BETTER, EVEN BLISSFUL MARRIAGE

January-February 1993

What makes a happy marriage? Commitment is the Christian's answer to a lasting marriage, and commitment can contribute to happiness, but what makes a rich, full blown relationship, full of peace and confidence?

Affection — freely bestowed, freely received, and freely returned. Well, you say, that's rare, and I think you are right, but we are talking here not of the norm, but what should and can be. Warm feelings, wisely expressed, give hope, encouragement, comfort.

A sense of humor. It's hard to be laughed at but we can learn to laugh with our spouse. Nothing is more satisfying to a couple than a mutual understanding of what is funny and an ability to treat particular matters lightly; that is, not important enough to precipitate a crisis. What a privilege for children to see this ease of manner and pleasure in their parents.

Absence of gossip. A friend of many years said to me of her husband "Why, I can't even carry on a decent conversation with him because he won't talk about anyone." Her tongue is often in her cheek, and she and I both appreciate his refusal to gossip. We are relieved of immense burdens when there is no hurtful conversation in the home. Both parents and children are winners, and there is beauty all around.

No manipulation. How easy it is to "work" a husband or a wife. And how tempting if we want our own way. If we can't be open and honest and submissive to each other, the greatest happiness on earth becomes a morass of suspicion, nagging, coveting, dissatisfaction, complaining.

Simple lives. In recent months, a number of Christians have testified to the increased joy in their homes because of simplifying their life styles. Even when we are very sure we cannot spend less, it can be fun to keep closer accounts and discover together how a few or many dollars can be saved. Schedules can also be reduced. Home life is improved when family members discover each other.

Encouragement. Our biggest booster should be our mate. What a joy to hear that the food was good or that the new bathroom shelf is wonderful. But what about being told that it is great to live with someone who just turned forty — or sixty — and that he wouldn't trade these years for anything? What bliss!

Jean Belz

When a house is a home

March-April 1993

I wonder why memories of our old house don't go away. Do they mean something significant in the life I now live? It was a rented house, much to the chagrin of my father who wanted a place of his own for his family.

A row of large white birches bordered the street. Each tree seemed to have a personality as did the evergreens on the lawn — low, accessible branches, easy to climb, friendly — or resistant, scratchy, unsatisfactory — or always unfamiliar, unapproachable, to be passed unnoticed. The front porch, a few steps up from the sidewalk, was a place to stomp off snow in the winter and to sit and talk in the summer. I believe we carried chairs in and out for the grown-ups. I don't recall lawn chairs or mosquito repellent. My sisters and I sat close together on the steps. Politics was regularly discussed, but the younger children often recited poems and sang songs for an eager audience.

The front door opened into the dining room. The only constant about the number at the table was that it was always full. There were eight of us to begin with, and my father frequently brought home a guest — a salesman, a German-speaking friend, or perhaps a down-and-outer. My mother was accommodating if not always enthusiastic. Even the plainest food that my mother cooked tasted good. The old mission oak furniture, in demand nowadays, served us well.

An open stairway led from the dining room to the upstairs bedrooms. Off the farthest bedroom was a sleeping porch, screened, not windowed, facing the street. I cannot imagine settling four or five lively youngsters for bed so publicly, but we were cool at night, leisurely in the morning, and energetic all day. Stairs led from this same room to the attic where we children presented wonderful dramas, mostly original, to anyone who would come. These efforts ended with patrons and cast alike weak from laughing no matter the theme of the production.

Bay windows with deep seats were interest centers in the living and dining rooms. Here were house plants important to both father and mother. One end of a seat was just right for stacking birthday or Christmas gifts for a day or two. The seats were airports for my brother who set up flight schedules for a fleet of toy planes and somehow drafted me. Perhaps this was the time he arranged for me to learn the Morse code. And we all gathered at the window seat to take our turns at the crystal radio set — more than seventy-five years ago. Probably the piano corner was the busiest. My father in his oak rocker, reading Will Rogers, and my mother in hers, darning socks, weren't just tolerant but encouraging as we practiced lessons, sang hymns, or waxed operatic on "The Student Prince" or "The Desert Song."

My parents' bedroom was off the living room so that my sisters and I always had to decide whether or not it was worth it to go from our far upstairs room through the hall, down the stairs, and through the dining and living rooms to report an earache or a bad dream.

The bathrooms are not to be mentioned except to say there was a painted tin tub that would not hold paint. This did not prevent my mother from insisting that her four blonde girls always emerge from the house "neat and clean with shiny hair" or from taking in a waif now and then and giving him a good scrubbing.

How could the kitchen be so inadequate and yet do the job? There was barely room to pass as we walked by the cook stove with cobs and coal, but bread rose on the warming oven doors, water got hot in the reservoir, we sometimes sat on the open oven door to get warm, we popped corn, made fudge, perked coffee, and enjoyed delicious meats, vegetables and desserts cooked on that old stove.

And my mother ironed in the kitchen, often after we had gone to bed, as my father sat and talked with her. A vivid memory is going downstairs for a drink of water and finding my parents making a pattern of creases in the ironing board cover and arguing about it. About what, I wondered. About the floor plan of a house they hoped to build some day.

When the old becomes new

May-June 1993

I listened to a good friend relating the beginning of his Christian experience: he was a young man and had received Christ as his Savior sometime earlier. Now as he sat and talked with friends, he thought, "There must be more than this." What a positive and happy conclusion!

Of course, we can go to our graves with the name Christian but with lives as sterile and purposeless as if we had never heard of Christ. And I suppose that was the way I was headed. Having gone through the strains of the Depression besides growing up in a household full of ups and downs, I envisioned an orderly life for myself. I looked forward to a rewarding career, perhaps in some sort of library work, marriage to a successful and sensitive man, and several exemplary children. I surely intended to work hard in the PTA and to enjoy a literary club. Symphony concerts and travel were part of my plans. A rich and full home life based on the values I had been taught as a child were a natural part of my thinking.

And most of these desires came my way, albeit some very modestly. However, I am thankful to say, the Lord stopped me short when I was still a young woman and showed me, as He did my friend, that these pleasures were not enough. There was more.

How many PTA meetings must one attend to make a dent in the education woes of the world? How many Little League games does it take to balance a child's life? How many piano lessons must a child take to gain satisfaction for his soul? No pursuit in the world is more worthwhile than education — in the church, in the school, and in the home. There is no more joyful discipline in the home than music, especially in piano or singing. But when the Lord Jesus Christ took away my nagging sin that tarnished every earthly thing, He gave meaning to every experience. There was purpose in concerts, books, friendships, school, politics, travel, efforts of many kinds. The world about me was different. Colors were deeper; textures, shapes, and distances took my attention. The faces of my family became more dear to me, and their response in expression and word was vital, sweet. My husband and children, whether successful and exemplary or not in the eyes of the world, have, by God's grace, brought me every happiness. Fullness and satisfaction are in Jesus.

Believing what you're doing is right – sticking with it

July-August 1993

When the word *continuity* was brought to mind recently, I thought, "Of course, that's it. That's the key."

Many years ago when my husband was a student pastor, I headed up the vacation Bible school in our small church. I was a young Christian and inexperienced. Nothing about the situation pointed toward establishing any continuity. We were barely hanging on. Among the junior highers that I taught was a young girl from a large family in need of the gospel. After a day or two of trying to teach what I had prepared, I pitched it all and fell back on God's plan of salvation and his dealings with the Israelites as I had recently come to understand them. By God's grace this took hold.

Life-long relationships were built. All kinds of problems and struggles ensued, but my young friend and her siblings were a hardy and engaging lot and not easy to resist. Through the years there have been marriages, children born, deaths, misunderstandings, and reconciliations. Outstanding gifts and skills have developed among the family members, but, best of all, many of them have a ready testimony to the saving power of Christ. There are numerous children and grandchildren, and I am privileged to teach some of the fourth generation in the schoolroom every day.

Is this important? Is it worth it? Of course. Could someone else have ministered to this family? Again — of course. But we were here, and they have ministered to us in turn. A friend wrote to me that she was able to go into the home of a sick neighbor and tidy the kitchen. Years earlier someone had done the same thing for her. Without any hope of returning the first favor, she was now able to pass it on, to continue the kindness.

Even if we should move a long distance away or suffer sickness or death or loss, we may still have some of our familiar things to enjoy, but, more important, we have our way of thinking, our values to live by. Suddenly we are surprised with their worth.

Not even big changes necessarily interrupt continuity. I think it isn't something we work hard at. It is a faithfulness, believing what we're doing is right, worth sticking with. There is a rush of comfort in tying the present to the past. A student asked me one day, "Why do we always have boiled eggs, orange juice, and homemade cinnamon rolls on Sunday morning?" Well, I certainly didn't set out 60 years ago to continue such a custom till now, but at that time, after mopping up spills and changing shirts before the day had scarcely begun, I declared sticky milk off the menu. If a thing is good, there's every reason to continue.

Jean Belz

Simply exciting

September-October 1993

We were preparing a table for a number of guests, and my granddaughter was rummaging through my rather dubious silver supply in an attempt to make each place setting uniform even if they didn't all match each other. Suddenly she chuckled and said, "There. They came out just right. The Lord did that."

I was digging for twelve pink napkins and hoping that they would be just right with the old pink tablecloth. My heart gave a little leap. "That's the way it should be," I said happily. "To know that the Lord is in it and brings everything together is what makes housekeeping — or anything else — a pleasure and worthwhile."

So many details of our lives are significant. The change in seasons is delightful. On September 21 I can be sure I'm looking straight west as I watch the sun set. Before that, it has been up north, and now it moves steadily to the south, so I know very well, as it travels down into the southwest horizon, there will be cold days ahead. But only for a few months, and during that time I can marvel at the beauty of the bare-branched trees against the rosy evening sky. The cold facts of science are full of purpose and joy.

The prism in the window throwing colors about the room, fresh grape jelly standing jewel-like on the counter, a grandson plopping his music onto the piano ready to play, a granddaughter declaring the third stanza of a certain hymn her very most favorite, or a shelf full of books to examine and read — the very thought of it all is exciting.

My husband often remarked, at the table, that we were eating blessed food. But isn't the family down the road enjoying blessed food? Yes, if the Lord is honored in their eating. We belong to a group that enjoys special privileges, but the group is not exclusive; anyone who wants to can get in.

Jean Belz

The greatness of language

November-December 1993

According to a recent newspaper article, findings indicate that language may be innate, not acquired or perhaps developed from some primitive sort of sound. The writer offered supporting statements, but they are not requisite to my belief that language is a gift from God. The very One who gave us language, who gave Adam the wisdom to name all of the animals, is the Word. The Apostle John tells us, "In the beginning was the Word, and Word was with God, and the Word was God." When this same Word, the Lord Jesus Christ, was tempted by the Devil in the wilderness, His response three times began: "It is written."

Consider the verb *to be* or, in the Latin, *sum.* I tell students we must have such a word because it means existence. When David killed Goliath, he was serving a living God. When Moses asked God who he should say was sending him, the Lord said, "I Am That I Am." Sometimes when I ask Korean or Spanish or Amharic speaking students what the verb for "is" or "be" is in their language, they reply that there isn't a word like that. But when I ask how they say, "I am sick," and then, "He is sick," they quickly understand the slight difference in the forms. The verb *to be* is essential.

And think of prefixes! First of all, we have hundreds and hundreds of marvelous Latin and Greek roots — strong roots that express strong actions, deep pathos, creative, imaginative thoughts. But they aren't so rigid that the sense of them can't be changed by prefixes like *ad*, *ab*, *con*, *de*, and *per*. What a pleasure to know how to convey our ideas in simple–or complicated–words, sentences, and paragraphs. A young teacher once exclaimed to me, "I love grammar! You have to account for every word in a sentence. It's better than Scrabble!"

And the verb tenses are dramatic. So much hinges on them. Yet we use them so freely, we are scarcely aware of their power. For example, we learn that the perfect tenses mean action completed. And then we read of Christ's perfect work on the cross, and we see action completed in the best sense possible. We can read and speak and write, and the words make pictures in our mind's eye. This is a high privilege and a precious gift, not to be trampled down or tossed away.

Jean Belz

Keep On

January-February 1994

The hour between the Sunday morning worship service and the afternoon meal is the loneliest and the choicest of the week. Do you have an hour like this? It may be so cloudy and dark that the weather comes right down to my shoe tops. Or it might be so dazzling and sunny, as today, that campus buildings are glistening white. Returning home, I open my front door and step out of the loveliness of the blue sky, the white snow, and the bare browns and grays of the trees and into my warm living room, I am comforted but tentative. Shall I make a cup of coffee and read a little while or write a letter? I refuse to let the television interrupt this solitude. Shall I play the piano, and if I do, shall I play hymns or Mozart? I'd like to take a second cup from the cupboard and have someone enjoy the outdoor beauty with me from my windows.

I wonder if this is a good time to look again at recent snapshots of my grandchildren? Am I becoming inhospitable? In past years, I prepared the afternoon meal, and every comer was a guest at our table. At 74, have I lost my identity? I'm concerned I'm self-serving, not sacrificial. But I am comforted when folks say, "You've had your turn." Or when my children warmly invite me to "come be where [they are]."

But the treasured time is almost gone. The afternoon and the week beckon. I must prepare the snack for the students tonight. I have new books to read. Shopping and errands must be done. Even my income tax seems inviting, to say nothing of the seed catalogs. Classes begin tomorrow with the pleasant prospect of leading youngsters in every area of their lives. There will be concerts and weddings and ball games and banquets. The door will open and the phone will ring.

But right now, no door slams and no phone rings.

Jean Belz

Some things don't change

March-April 1994

There surely was soda pop in the 1920s in some quarters, but it was a rare item at our house. Regularly on Wednesdays my sisters and I were given five cents each, and again on Saturdays. We spent those nickels with so much confidence, so much satisfaction, on ice cream lollipops (handmade at the drug store) or on frozen chocolate bars. Pop was never a consideration. Even now, a six-pack on the basement step or in the back hall spells indolence, waste. My prudent mother would not have endured a can of soda left here or there half drunk and lukewarm.

But sometimes on a picnic or on a trip, the sky was the limit. There in front of a gasoline station would often be the sign: "We Don't Know Where Mom Is, But Pop's In The Cooler." Such sentiment was utterly distasteful to my mother, but niceties were unimportant at such a moment. "Decide. Make up your mind," Dad would say. And I would waveringly pass by the orange — always good but too common, the strawberry — so temptingly fizzy, the cream soda — so grown-up, and make my selection — grape! Cool. Rich. Purple.

I grew up. I learned to like coffee, strong and hot, and iced tea, refreshing, stimulating. No sweet drink would ever again appeal. Or would it? I was 44 years old and leaving South Carolina for home in Iowa. The spring air was heavy with fragrance as the train ran through a fairyland of blossoms from Greenville to Atlanta. The car on the Southern Railway was warm. As I opened the sandwich my daughter had carefully made — thin-sliced ham with homemade bread — I asked the porter what I could drink. "What you want with that sandwich," he said, "is a bottle of grape." How did he know?!

And now I am 71, preparing to take an automobile trip with grandchildren for the third time. Will I hold out? Can I drive all that way? Will these two granddaughters be as compatible as my grandsons were two years ago? What clothes do I need for the Southwest? Will I remember my coffee? Which girl should serve the crackers and cheese and apples for lunch? I'm a tiny bit edgy. Of course, we'll stop for rest rooms and gasoline and drinks. We'll look for a nice place so that we can get everything . . . perhaps film or a magazine or aspirin. And then I'll just walk over to that big glass door, open it, look quickly down the rows of flavors, and I'll choose grape.

Jean Belz

A woman's life, liberty and pursuit of happiness

September-October 1994

It has occurred to me that I'm a little different from many others in my "pursuit of happiness," but that there is a sort of intangible something that slows the pursuit and makes clear the happiness. What could have contributed to the peace of mind and deep down joy of a head-strong girl who was born bossy and who never liked to take orders? When I was given to moods, how did I maintain any kind of cheerful balance? The truth is I was transformed by the mercy of Christ.

In our home older brothers helped younger sisters to be competitive and enjoy it; they were even sometimes admiring and always respectful. Our father was demanding, not indulgent, but we were sure he thought we were special, capable, able to hold our own. And marriage, eight children, and years of hard work only enhanced this experience. By God's grace I was privileged. With such a desirable position solidly established, why would a woman not be satisfied.

My husband once suggested that since others in our little print shop were signing time cards and receiving a modest wage, I might like to do the same for the proofreading and the editing, or even for the "sweeping out"

I did on late work nights. It held no appeal no matter how generous the pay might be. I could think of no amount that would be enough, and my husband understood. I was happy to be free to enjoy my housekeeping, my children, and the proofreading.

But things are different nowadays. So it seems that a woman should be free to enjoy a job if she likes — or even if the need is thrust upon her. And she may manage beautifully without chafing or raising any sort of strident voice. Another may rejoice in a simple life and spending all her time on responsibilities in the home. Sometime ago a young mother told me that as she was driving her children to school one day she suddenly realized it wasn't something else she wanted — it was singing children, a loving husband, a meaningful life. I can hear now my father say in his German brogue, "If you don't have contentment, you have nothing."

What a blessing when resentment toward our circumstances does not prevail! Not long ago one of my sons said to me, "Mom, you were always liberated." And I was.

Jean Belz

Don't worry. Your strength shall be in measure.

November-December 1994

A few days ago a small grandson asked me how many meetings were held, over the years, in the round-roofed building, our recently vacated chapel. Well, subtract 49 from 94. That is 45 years times 52 weeks times four meetings a week, and that is 9370. And that doesn't count extra meetings and daily school chapels. That's what church buildings are for. The responsibilities that fall on all church congregations were carried out here in spite of the simple, homemade structure.

Widely known church leaders spoke here on vital issues. From their early married years till they were grandparents, missionaries from all over the world came and went. Several politicians with Christian testimonies have spoken to us. Preacher after preacher has visited bearing the gospel. And our own pastors faithfully delivered the truth of the Scriptures. Besides all this, graduation exercises, Christmas programs, choir concerts, weddings, and funerals have brought standing-room-only audiences.

Even so, as I sat in a front pew at most of these

meetings, I sometimes sat with agitated heart. "Is the kitchen tidy? Is the roast big enough? Did the boys find their clean shirts? Should the baby be in church with that cough? Will my husband remember all of the announcements? Is his sermon theme too narrow? Did he pray too long?" And occasionally I sat with rebellious heart — "If I have to sit and look out that church screen door one more time, I can't bear it! Why am I here? This isn't what I planned for my life!" But I don't remember a time when my heart wasn't calmed, not by any sort of magic, but by the Lord's loving faithfulness in quieting a foolish, troubled heart.

A yellow birch was just beyond the church screen door across the rough drive. In season, a yellow iris bloomed at the base of the tree. In the distance was the farmhouse. Sometimes a latecomer to church stepped in and out of view. Sometimes a dog or a cat skulked by as if it knew full well it was missing the meeting. The screen door view was not always satisfactory. But back in the pews from week to week, lives were changed and the Lord kept things real.

Just in time — just as the ceiling tile under the round roof began to fall in earnest — the new chapel was ready — not a separate building with bricks and rest rooms and offices — but what will be the library — hence the Library-Chapel. Now I sit in a large, high ceilinged, white-walled room with lovely, tall, narrow corner windows. If I raise my eyes, beautiful glimpses of green lawn or white snow, young trees, the drive in the distance flick in and out of my vision. And the hearts of younger women are being calmed as their husbands preach. Students are finding hope in Christ, a young mother determines to live for Him, and whole families find Him sufficient. The good news is the same.

A short history of trains

January-February 1995

The romance of the railroads calls for recording recollections before they fade away completely. I don't want to lose vivid memories or even fuzzy ones.

Several trunks and bags were sitting on the brick platform at the railroad station in our tiny town ready to be shoved into the baggage car. My sister was off for nurse's training and we were saying good-bye. I was five. In those days my father frequently "rode the caboose" when he shipped a load of cattle to Chicago. And I recall a Thanksgiving Day when my father brought the cook on a section crew home for dinner. It was a sort of busman's holiday for the cook because he exchanged recipes with my mother and helped us wash the dishes.

In my childhood we frequently met trains, but I never boarded one. I was ten when I went with my father and mother to visit Mr. Ralph Budd, a high school teacher of my mother's and then a well known railroad executive, in his private car. I wanted to go around the world in that railroad car. Luxury abounded and excitement gripped me. Sometimes an uncle and aunt arrived by train from the East or from the West. Their ease regarding train travel, not on just one continent, but two, was mystifying and enviable. Some years later a paralyzing snowstorm spoiled the long anticipated drive home from college at spring break, but the trains ran, and I was soon safe at home.

Our wedding trip was by train, an early streamliner, rushing us into Chicago and a big hotel on the lakefront, museums, restaurants, plays, shopping, churches, and back again to establish our home. Those days began to close the Depression era.

And so the list seems almost too meager to go on. Yet the trips that followed were significant: on the Rocket, the Great Western, or the Burlington to the Twin Cities we felt glad for a seat (actually guilty if a soldier stood and we sat).

Sometimes we took the Illinois Central to Chicago and changed trains there to go to Cleveland. Our second grader rode the Illinois Central with her classmates from Independence, Iowa, to Manchester, thirty miles away, for an outing with her teacher. When she was eleven, she left the same station to begin a trip to Philadelphia. And on a dark, bitter, snowy morning my sister boarded at that station to begin a trip that would take her to Jordan for seven years as a missionary nurse.

Students returned from visits home to the Chicago area on the Northwestern. Late at night when we thought we had collected everyone possible, the phone would ring and a forlorn voice would say, "I'm at the Ham and Egger. I just got off the train." Off we went again.

Great satisfaction accompanied a trip to St. Louis on the Rock Island, on to Atlanta on the L&N, and finally to Greenville, South Carolina, on the Southern Railway. There was a new grandchild in Greenville. Who wouldn't be satisfied? But the trip itself was efficient and delightful.

It was a great pleasure to my husband to make business trips to St. Louis on the Rocket, boarding in Cedar Rapids in the evening and arriving in St. Louis about breakfast time. The train left St. Louis again about five p.m. On one occasion my husband and a friend and I were enjoying our dinner in the small diner as we wound north, glimpsing the Mississippi now and then. When I ordered a pot of coffee, our frugal friend insisted that we get one pot and divide it. I was dubious. But I agreed, and the pot, a very small one, arrived. Our friend raised his eyebrows in some consternation and asked the waiter, "How much does that pot hold?" "A cup and a half," the waiter answered with a smile. "Why, on the Great Northern," our friend sputtered, "you get two cups and a half." Again with a smile, the waiter replied, "That's what makes 'em great."

About thirty years ago our younger children took the train on a special farewell trip from Center Point to Oelwein, Iowa. There was ice cream at the other end. Now there are only flowering crabs and sumac on that railroad bed. But — take heart — there is Amtrak ahead — and Sacramento — and Seattle — and home again.

I "used to"

March-April 1995

What do you mean when you say *used to*? Doesn't it mean that you did something enough times that it became quite familiar to you? Did you do it over and over for awhile? Perhaps it left pleasant memories. Isn't it usually something you were fond of doing? — My brother and sisters and I used to play the piano and sing together. We used to hike down the railroad track. We used to have cold beef sandwiches for Sunday night supper. We used to live in northwest Iowa.

Well, it was jarring when a friend told me she used to go swimming with a family and they used to buy ice cream cones — and I then discovered that they had gone swimming for just one day and had bought ice cream on just one day. That was it. What kind of thinking is that? What conception of time?

Then we took Amtrak to Sacramento, from there to Eugene, and from Seattle home, with cars and buses in between. As we anticipated, trying to sleep in the coach or to sightsee in the rain was miserable, but a sense of being lifted up and out of our ordinary lives easily eclipsed the misery. There we were — in the midst of the people we see every day, enjoying the pleasures of the train as if it were ours, as if it were no surprise — and yet we were awed. Imagine glancing across the dining car and seeing two of our own junior high boys seated at a table with white cloth and fresh flowers ordering hamburgers.

The strangeness of the lights of the cities didn't matter. We were on to the next stop. Mile after mile revealed lakes and rivers, mountains and canyons, buildings, bridges, forests, and beaches. How came we there? Suddenly we had been marvelously transported, set down in new places, and wonderfully provided for. On all sides loving friends, growing churches, and busy schools appeared at just the right time. Best of all, the students stepped up time after time and sang beautifully and confidently.

Time to be thoughtful and consider these blessings from the Lord. The train rounded Puget Sound at the supper hour. The sun made a golden path on the shining water. It was night as we crossed Washington state. We woke up to the grandeur of Glacier National Park. On the second morning, headed east, we followed the Mississippi from St. Paul to LaCrosse. The loveliness of Wisconsin hills matched any beauty we had seen.

The first few days at home brought sweet remembrance. When I asked fellow travelers if they enjoyed the trip, they said, "Oh, yes!" When I asked, "Would you go again?" the answer was the same. And in my musings and memories, I must admit to thinking, with some longing, "I used to eat in the diner."

Family tapestry unfolds at reunions

May-June 1995

I have recently come from a reunion with my siblings — five of us in our seventies. It is remarkable that circle has not been broken. Next came the cousins — all delighted to see each other — and their children after them. And those little children! Babies and toddlers looking as if some wonderful hand had stamped out one fine child after another. Hasn't this been your experience? And, of course, God's wonderful hand has done it — not carelessly, but with all knowledge and love.

Freedom looked to be within the grasp of the six- to ten-year-olds who reported in only now and then to settle a quarrel or seek solace in a Band-aid. They looked up from their play, not the least bit surprised, to see relatives from hundreds of miles away — as if everyone lived next door to each other the year round. And the twelve-year-olds seemed not to report in at all, except for meals. Did one grandson really eat seven cinnamon rolls, or did the ducks at the dock get some? And is this the same grandson exhibiting model behavior as he meets his great uncle?

The patience and willing spirit of the high schoolers and college students are a curious pleasure. Is helping tend younger cousins and talking with their elders real to them, or are they simply marking time until they are in school again with friends and studies? Do they need encouragement, or is their confidence enough? A grandmother is much pleased with their attractiveness and capabilities and determines not to be doting.

Will anyone go home saying, "It's too bad Johnny hasn't done better," or, "I don't know why Pete hasn't been harder on Jim"? I don't think so. There's something about being a spouse and a parent that fosters more compassion and understanding for one another. Our grown-up children are in charge. They have enormous responsibilities. They don't listen to us as much as in former years. (This is a little puzzling because, often times, I'm sure I know more than they do.) Their careers are important, but their families are more so. Praise God when the two make for a happy and harmonious home.

If you are not caring for children now, your own or someone else's, I hope you find a way to enjoy this precious privilege.

To the trees

July-August 1995

In the midst of the refurbished houses, the gardens, the flowers, the bookshelves, the mowed lawns, the soccer fields, the books, the weddings, the vacations, the collared shirts — all clamoring for and getting our attention — there are the trees. What a balm! What a wonder!

They came to us looking like small sticks — all 2000 of them. They were planted in a four-acre area, according to instructions, by hardworking, earnest men and boys, but not experts. There were many kinds — oak, ash, maple, pine, cedar, plum, and spruce. A rainy season helped and a good stand resulted. But there were weeks of wondering which would win out — the trees or the grass. Helpers dug to find the tiny shoots and they weeded in the rows. Students tied pink ribbons on the seedlings to warn the mower. Crews placed short lengths of tile around the slender trunks. One girl was assigned to find all of the evergreens in the northernmost rows. If one wondered where to find the project "foreman," he was almost sure to be "in the trees." Each stage of growth seemed more promising than the last.

Three years have passed. There is no shade yet, unless you stand close on the north side of a tree, but several maples are well over head-high. In the summer two young boys were regularly off "to the trees" to snip off lower branches. A rascally rabbit persisted in snipping off a few of his own, but the small oaks he chose grew right back. The red-winged blackbirds fuss when we unwittingly go near their homes.

And oh, the walks! Where to walk? To the trees, of course. We can choose our path, eight feet wide and newly mowed. The sun is dropping down enough to give everything a deep color. I think I like best to walk from east to west. Shall I examine the maples tonight or take a closer look at the thriving spruce? If the children run away from us, they're all right. It's safe here. And there are others walking too. Two women in the far path are so intent on their conversation, we don't exchange greetings. No need to. One path should be named esplanade, a beautiful word. It is so wide and inviting. As we spread out on it, we meet a couple, and immediately the conversation is light, relaxed, and delightful. I feel transported to scenes from Jane Austen whose characters daily found joy, and sadness, too, in their walks. How can one place, at the same time, lend itself to such public and private pleasure? This is a special gift from the Lord. Come and take a walk.

That feeling of inadequacy

September-October 1995

I think I'd rather be inadequate than incompetent. But why, if they mean the same thing? An inadequacy seems to let me down a little more gently than an incompetency. If I'm inadequate, I'm weak and undeserving, but if I'm incompetent, I feel accused. Have you ever had an inkling that you failed at a task because you were inadequate? Have you thought to yourself, "If you knew you couldn't do it, why did you take it on?" In the face of such discouragement, I begin to wonder how much of all my work is dubious because I'm inadequate. But we can't sit whimpering, hoping for some indulgent person to buoy us up. Better to ask, "Why did I take it on?"

Well, there's an up side. I am inclined to take the high road and attempt things whether I'm an expert or not. Besides that, some responsibilities are thrust on one. Years ago several students appeared unexpectedly as the school year opened, all desirable and all eager to be guided and taught. A sense of ineffectiveness gripped me, but I couldn't say, "I'm inadequate. Go away." Instead, we took them on with a good amount of success. And we can capitalize on our strengths. We may be forced to admit to failure now and then, but we can keep our chins up when we do well even in very small matters. My favorite show of confidence comes from a friend of long ago. We were chatting about sundry affairs when she said, "I baked bread today. It was unusually good. But then, it usually is." I was set back a little. But she was just sure of herself — or, at least, of her bread.

A long look back across the years helps us deal with our weaknesses and abilities. But if we must wait for old age to have enough wisdom to attempt the challenges that come our way, what poor lives we lead. Our inadequacies belong with the Lord who strengthens us.

Lifetime's book of quotations

November-December 1995

My friend across the fields, years ago, saw a rabbit in her garden, and — said she — "I threw on my jacket, picked up my gun, and went out and shot it." Such dispatch! If I wanted to take such action, my jacket would never be on the hook, and if I had a gun, I wouldn't shoot straight.

When she came to help us, she came on "shank's ponies" (no car that day), and as she opened the paint can, she declared, "Paint covers a multitude of sins."

Another friend, in the same peer group, would often look with discouragement at a job and say "I wish it was done." I thought he meant that was the next job to be done, but, no, his family said. He meant he "wished it was done." In a lighter mood, when a board was too long, he would say, "Don't know what to do. If it was too short, we could splice it."

Much earlier in my life, as the wind all but blew us away, our neighbor would say, "The north end of that south wind gets pretty cold sometimes." This seemed perfectly reasonable to me, and somehow I could envision myself getting fairly comfortable in the curve of the wind, always avoiding the north end. Our neighbor was a tall, gaunt man with a wide, black moustache and a quizzical smile. When we stopped in his kitchen on a warm summer night, he was stretched out on a kitchen chair, dressed in overalls with no shirt and with bare feet. With a big spoon he was eating something smooth and white from a very large mixing bowl cradled in his lap, dashing a little sugar on each slippery spoonful. "Clabber," he offered, at our wonderment. (Nowadays we'd call it yogurt — in big supply.) It seemed to me that our friend represented everything that was comfortable and cool and free.

I treasure time spent with a busy housewife, absolutely self-sacrificing, who apologized for "always coming up from behind." Why wouldn't she "come up from behind" when she waited on everyone in sight?

The mother of a young friend was usually humming hymns as she worked about her home. Now and then she would softly sing the words. I wanted to edge closer to her, to find out about her quiet spirit and what the songs meant to her. I heard a grandmother tell her grandson when she was about to make a dubious choice, "We have to live with ourselves, you know." My own mother always insisted, "Be sure you are neat and clean," and my father often said "If you don't have contentment, you've got nothing."

How rich I am with this heritage. Surely there were

negative influences, but they seem to have faded. Even in my adulthood my grandmother often cautioned, "Child, don't run. Walk." Well, I'm walking now, and it gives me time to remember.

Jean Belz

Saving grace

January-February 1996

When I was much younger, a well-known columnist mentioned that her mother-in-law had given her a ten-dollar bill and told her to keep it in her purse against a rainy day. If a rainy day required it, she was to replace it as soon as possible. I decided to do the same thing for one of my daughters-in-law, and she took kindly to the idea. In thinking it over, I now can hear my other four daughters-in-law, and, for that matter, my own three daughters asking why they were never so guided. Perhaps they were far away; or perhaps I never had seven more ten dollar bills. The one recipient has probably long since forgotten being indulged in this way.

Well, I took the suggestion for myself and it has been a great comfort. "But," you say, "ten dollars is nothing." And you are almost right, but if it were something, I couldn't keep it. I would need it. This way, I'm always devising ways of not spending it. Often the best part is that I don't need it, but someone else does, and there it is — to be used — and replaced.

Another daughter-in-law leaves to go on a little shopping binge now and then, quietly returning with a few quality gifts and several articles of clothing for the family. All agog, the rest of us — we know she is not loaded with this world's goods — ask her how she did it. "Well, I found some money tucked in a drawer," she answers modestly. She found it there because she tucked it there.

I once read that we can't save unless we say "no" to something we can do without. And then when we think we have resisted all we can, we say "no" again, and finally we say it again. It sounds like a cruel process — no fun — but it is freeing, satisfying. You may say, "It doesn't sound very generous to me, not very open-handed." But it's far better than reaching into an empty pocket.

It's a microcosm of the big picture that is the story of our lives. If a child is given a twenty-five cent piece, can he give five cents to the Lord, save ten cents and spend ten cents? Of course. Can he continue to handle his money in these proportions? Probably not. But can he spend less than he makes? I'm sure he usually can. How blessed we are to give those gifts that we have laid up in store. What joy to work with our hands to have to give to one in need.

Jean Belz

Doors

March-April 1996

One of my sons said recently that he was glad that we opened a number of doors of interest for him but never forced him to go through. Maybe we should have. He might now be more effective in his work or more sure of himself or more exacting in detail. And he might not. The niche or niches in which he now finds himself seem to fit so well.

What courage it takes for a parent to guide and discipline a child and still keep hands off. Or for a teacher as he considers the student and longs for his success. What a temptation it is to drive a youngster to use certain of his gifts in such a way that he finally has nowhere to turn. Or to press him with financial means to persuade him to our point of view.

I have dreamed of organizing a neat little packet of hobbies and, as the youngsters come to school, dropping the students, one at a time, into the slots, and telling them to succeed. That doesn't work. They will soon move toward the jobs or pastimes that interest them. And they should. In order to exhibit any vitality, a student must seek the job himself and establish himself in it. Doesn't he get any help or advice? Of course, if he wants it and especially if he should do wrong. But we soon discover the baby-sitters, the carpenters, the electronics experts, the outdoor people, the tutors, the cooks, the cleaners, the artists. They become students who are valued and sought out.

Now and then I hear that a youngster has gone off to college and no one has befriended him. This can happen. But the student can turn it all around by being a friend and forming a group of friends (making sure no one else is neglected). Adults can do this too. As Shakespeare's Henry the Fifth said to his new queen, "We are the makers of manners." Who better than Christians to set the pace?

I once assigned a class of fifth and sixth graders to write an essay on initiative. The essay was to include an example of the subject. The students didn't hesitate. One of the boys wrote that whenever his father poured a concrete feeding floor on their farm, he designed it so that a building could be placed on it if desired. Another boy said that when their very large family arrived home in the evening with their mother, she immediately gave every child a job, and they soon had a good supper on the table. However accurate the students were, they sensed that initiative meant seeing something to be done and doing something about it.

How strong and happy the child who is allowed and urged to find his own talent, to build initiative, and, instead of expecting to be ministered unto, to minister.

Jean Belz

Scaling the mountains (of clutter)

May-June 1996

As I came in from the garden, the soft rain closed over me. I would be wet before I got to the house. I had been prudently digging dandelions out of the strawberries — with a genuine dandelion digger purchased for ten dollars — and the bed looked nice, white with bloom. Still, there were weeds here and there. I wish I could have gotten them all. My indignation rose. What a half-way business — the garden wasn't weed-free and I was getting soaked.

And at my sewing machine I wailed again. Here was a clutter of buttons, thread, needles, tape — all out of order. A half-finished skirt lay nearby along with two magazines turned to unfinished articles. I want my sewing to be neat, ready to take up again, and my reading to be organized so that I can say, "Oh, yes, I read that last night." I want to remember what some reputable person said on the subject.

It's the same in the kitchen. Instead of boasting a beautifully clear counter (like that of one of my dear relatives) I see on mine an apple or two and some bananas, at least one bouquet from the garden, one or two phone messages, a new picture of a grandchild or school child — all things I fear will be out of mind if I put them out of sight — or things I simply like to look at.

On to correspondence and writing. This should be satisfying, but things are everywhere — pens, note cards, yellow pads, clippings, stamps, scissors, letters, bills, checkbook, and consequently, my thoughts. Is it a lost cause? I want to do better, and I will, but I won't change much. Even our minds are cluttered sometimes, and we can't boast clear thinking or performance. God, in His mercy, is our comfort and wisdom.

JEAN BELZ

WHEN A HOUSE IS TRULY A HOME

July-August 1996

Getting older doesn't necessarily exclude having to "eat one's words," although I like to think I'm a little more judicious than I was in my younger days. One of the most foolish statements I ever made (and more than once) is, "I would never want to live there!" I said that about a rickety old farmhouse, never dreaming there was the remotest possibility of our occupying it. In less than a year, our family of six had moved into it, thankful for a place to be and enjoying all of the exciting aspects of our new situation. We didn't entertain kings, but our guests were kingly, and on that farm our children came to know men and women from around the world.

As we drive along the interstate, far away on the side of a mountain is a lone house. How could we ever get there? Wouldn't it be a lonely life? Where does the family go to school or church? It's too far, too isolated. But what if I knew the family? What if it were my son's or my daughter's? We could get there, and we'd love every mile.

The old, refurbished houses in our county seat town are lovely, but if I don't know the owners, they often seem closed and forbidding. If I know them, I feel a kind of propriety as I walk in. And good friends may live in plainer homes, but there's a welcome there.

In our state many old farm houses have been replaced by modern homes, but a house we all value is more than a hundred years old with few changes in that time. Its worth is in the character of those inside.

As we pass the old row houses in cities like Milwaukee or Baltimore or try to find a particular house among the winding streets of a new subdivision, the homes have little significance for us unless a family we love live there, have struggled to buy it, have moved their very own things into it, or have experienced joy and sorrow there whose meaning far transcends walls and windows, stairways and floors. If there is a warm familiarity, noisy steps or silent doors and carpet make little difference.

A day or two ago we passed a little bungalow that we have passed hundreds of times. I used to know a little girl who lived there. Suddenly I noticed how old-fashioned and pretty the house was with late summer flowers growing around the tidy front steps. I wondered: Do they set the table at night? Do they use a fresh cloth or place mats? Is it a hot meal or a snack? Who is there? My mind begins to stretch over thousands and millions of homes.

But wait a minute. I can't do this. Instead, I'll

remember a friend's wise remark, "The Lord knew what He was doing when He made the family." Families live in fortresses, and opportunity and strength lie behind those doors.

Boys to enjoy and love

September-October 1996

When I mentioned writing about boys, someone asked, "As over against girls?" Never.

A healthy little boy, when he is born, gives every sign of being strong, friendly, curious, helpful – a pleasure. Why not keep him that way? Well, he gets into things and he is stubborn. He can't be left to himself. But he shows so much promise. A long time ago when a small boy of mine was suffering from some sort of misdemeanor, I said, "Don't worry. You will probably be a great man some day." He answered sorrowfully, "I don't think so." But you know he is; he isn't famous or rich, but he's a great man.

A mother must keep up her courage and believe in her boys even if she can't really trust them. They can't really trust themselves. But things are easier when we recognize this vulnerability. My husband loved the cartoon where the boy is shouting out the second-floor window: "I can't come out now. I'm having a man-to-man talk with mom."

What do we think of when we look back? Slivers, cookies, broken bones, dirty socks, bicycles, ball gloves, first crushes, drivers' licenses, haircuts — not beautiful but so wonderful. There are so many ways to abdicate — they all must be resisted if we want the joy of a boy.

What privileges he offers–handing him a stack of clean clothes, passing him a tissue when it is desperately needed, serving him fresh rolls, correcting a measure as he practices piano, sharing the basketball scores, making a small loan, agonizing with him over a disappointment in love, discovering together the answer to one of life's big problems right there in the Scriptures.

My vantage point from having had five sons, thirteen grandsons, seven great grandsons, and dozens of school boys to enjoy and love is hard to match.

Is there anything to equal this blessing?

Some girls, of course.

Thinking of diamonds

November-December 1996

The word *imagination* never seems to be used positively in the Scriptures. It is synonymous with stubbornness and, in fact, denotes the worst of willful sin. This is a wonderful warning to us not ever to think of ourselves in the place of God.

But I often say to a student, "Use your imagination." I even plead with him to do it. Now I see that I'm fairly safe, since Webster says the use of imagination to mean evil plan or scheme is obsolete. (I'm sure it is not so obsolete that thoughts do not sometimes run wild — with terrible results.) But I want the student to stretch his mind. Can't he risk something? What's going to become of him? Will he fail? What will this dull indifference do to him? Will he get by, perhaps even prosper? If he doesn't venture too much, he may get into a comfortable position and not have to budge.

But it won't be very exciting or productive. I once told a boy, discouraged with his studies, "Make associations. Take what you hear from the pulpit to the classroom. Take classroom ideas to the supper table . . ." Frustrated, he retorted, "Well, I wouldn't get anything done if I did all that." Wiser classmates rose to my defense, and he began to see that understanding and action can go together.

All around are people who don't commit themselves. I often long to be like them — to maintain silence — to say "Perhaps so" or "I don't know." What a safe existence. The longing never lasts. I'm off again to a life of excitement — and difficulties.

Sometimes, when a student refuses to take the plunge and answer, I recklessly ask, "If you were to meet the firing squad at dawn unless you answer, what would you say?" No answer. Instead, the student looks at me wonderingly, hopelessly. Or better yet, if he says, "I don't know," I love to quote a teacher-friend: "Well, if you did know, what would you say?" He is startled — he answers — and sometimes correctly.

There is gold in the hills. There are diamonds in our backyards. The textbooks are full of thrilling numbers, facts, and names. They are all related to the world around us. Just think.

Never on the shelf

January-February 1996

"And, Mom, you just sit on that chair over there." These were instructions to my friend whose family was busy on a building project. Her answer: "I will not sit on a chair as long as there is something I can do." Is she stubborn? A little, perhaps. Is the family thoughtful? No doubt, they are.

How do we oldsters give up responsibilities — and privileges — gracefully? If we sense we are losing our grip on jobs we've done for years, we can swallow some pride and occupy ourselves with things less demanding. But that can be a quick way for atrophy to set in. Better to suffer a painful moment now and then or a little embarrassment than to be motionless on the shelf.

That older person who maintains his dignity and is treated with dignity is blessed. He doesn't clamor to be included every time, but he often is. He toughs it out when he feels less than well, but enjoys needed rest. He gives into kindnesses and is thankful. A man once offered to share his umbrella with me and I demurred, saying, "I'm not an umbrella woman." Holding my arm firmly, he replied, "Well, I'm an umbrella man." Delightful lesson.

After a lifetime of feeding and selling a few calves at

a time, my father, in his old age, was raising a calf in a lot on the edge of town. Of course, the calf got out, and the neighborhood ladies were understandably enraged when their gardens and flower beds were trampled. I would have been, too. Everyone was against Dad. But one part of me kept thinking, "Isn't it about as easy to get the calf out of the flower bed as it would be to go to a nursing home and visit Dad in his wheel chair?"

We aren't all vigorous. Each day gives me more compassion for the weak, but we need to be challenged to do a little more, perhaps, than we think we can do. Reading, writing — even letters and notes — cooking, gardening, attending church services, welcoming children, grandchildren, and friends into our homes, and praying with and for others all help to keep us alive and alert. And through it all, as my granddaughter embroidered on a sampler, "Kindness helps."

The passing scene

March-April 1997

As I eat my lunch, a pickup truck is bouncing along our blacktop road. At first I scarcely notice it; it's not important. Then there's an awareness of changes – differences. Every vehicle is a reminder of someone or something. I'm impressed with the huge semi-truck that thunders along with grain from the elevator to the barge. How much does it haul in a day? Why is it going by at 11:00 in the morning? How long does it spend loading and unloading? I think of grain in boxcars, not semis. Sleek cars rush by, and a heavy cement truck seems to go just as fast. A yellow school bus hurries along. At this hour?

But the pickups prevail. They display a remarkably free spirit. They seem so practical, usable, although some writer has said that often they haul nothing – just the passengers in the cab. No doubt, that's urban. We're rural. The variety of loads is endless – tools, feed, lumber, paint, plants, trees, chickens, eggs (we borrowed one, long ago, for a goat), lawn mowers, picnic food, furniture.

But at noon? Is a farmer on a quick errand to town before lunch? Perhaps something broke down, or he's dashing to the bank. I finish my lunch a little sadly. He may eat in town. His wife may be at work in town. He may not have a wife. Fifty or sixty years ago I laboriously prepared a large noon-time meal every day. A close friend made a pie for her family each morning. They expected it. Those were not the days of cottage cheese and spinach at noon and calories at night.

Maybe these days are better than the old. Do we need that 12:00 hour? We do, for sure. We can put a quick note in the mail. We can eat lunch or not. We can take a short nap or read the daily paper. We can watch a sudden rainstorm come up. Or, if it is June, with its perfect, rare days, we can gaze at the heavens and listen to the words of "Silent Noon" by Dante Gabriel Rossetti:

> *"Deep in the sun-searched growths the dragon fly*
>
> *Hangs like a blue thread loosened from the sky."*

Change a bleak, busy, banging sort of hour to a few moments of loveliness as you see the quiet power of the sun at its height.

Power loss

May-June 1997

The words, in red, on the dashboard read "power loss." For a moment I felt only irritation, but then dread. Would I be delayed, or stranded till I was towed in, or, worse yet, would the car blow up? I suppose only a woman would worry about that. Years ago, when our car broke down and my husband suggested that "a rod had gone out," our daughter said impatiently, "Well, can't we put it back in?"

Power losses are not uncommon for me these days — my head, my feet, my back, my memory, my energy all fail me now and then. But there is power all around. How can those lilies make such a gorgeous display or those tomatoes and broccoli burst with goodness? How can the strawberry bed drip with luscious sweetness for a few weeks and then promptly stop — just in time for the raspberries to begin? How thankful I am that I can walk to the garden and wield a hoe or pick the peas.

And then I can drive to the little boys' baseball tournament! There are grandparents, parents, aunts, uncles, coaches, umpires and siblings supporting the teams. How did that nine-year-old learn to hit a home run or scoop up a line drive and throw it to first? And there are children everywhere — handsome children — small fry playing in the dirt, older ones eying one another to make new friendships, well dressed and well groomed young teenagers, and team members — some in new outfits and some in old shirts and shorts — waiting for their game. They all appear to be able to do anything. How hopeful it all seems. And yet I know there will be power losses along the way.

When I come home, I can go to the prayer meeting. I have often heard that is where the power of the church is. Take advantage of that energy. Pray in Jesus' name for daily bread, pray for health and peace, for the families at the ball game, for courage and wisdom. What power! In Christ, I count all losses gain.

Never a humdrum tablecloth

July-August 1997

Why do I fuss so about my tablecloths? The drawers aren't big enough and I can't stuff them all in. Well, I have found a fine storage box and it's a great satisfaction to lay each cloth, fresh from the laundry, neatly in it, wonderfully accessible for the next time.

It isn't as if I own beautiful tablecloths with fine china, glassware, and silver to match. Far from it. So why don't I discard some of them? Even now the yellow and white checked one is bright, not dingy, in spite of a few holes. It was one of my first long ones needed as the family grew to six, then eight children, even adding some friends' children coming to school. Another one, hand-woven from Mexico with a gray and white block pattern adorned with roses, is waiting now to have its frayed edges renewed. We got that one out when missionaries came or other guests, perhaps from New Zealand or Australia. We chose still another long one, again handwoven in a lovely hot pink with white, when we were very festive. If I put it on the table now, worn and thin, who can know the excitement of those early years?

The pleasure is still there when I take a stack of

sturdy, old, colorful square cloths, that don't match anything, out to the picnic tables. How fresh they look! How good the food tastes! Spills don't matter. And who remembers the yard-square linen cloths for luncheons at folding tables? Their cheerful embroidery and crocheted edges tell of an era long ago.

My earliest neighbor taught me to launder, dry, dampen, and then iron a long, white linen tablecloth, carefully folding the edges to the inside of the center crease so that the diners could see three beautiful creases atop the cloth. Marvelous! But it never became my practice. I would rather iron and use a lovely white cloth embroidered in rosebuds; even then busy days seem to preclude fussing.

Tablecloths from mothers-in-law may be common, but so are they from daughters-in-law and daughters as are several of my current ones. The bright green and white one and a beautiful, multi-colored one seem to say to me from the givers, "I knew you could still prepare something to serve on this cloth," or "I knew you would invite someone in for a meal served with this on your table." How encouraging!

When I was a young girl I visited in the home of an older friend. A small table was set simply but invitingly for supper. When we mentioned guests, she said, "Oh, it's just Charlie" — her husband. How can we do better than to seat a husband, children, parents, family, friends–and strangers–at our table, not grudgingly but as a privilege? We'll be eating blessed food.

Keeping Objective

September-October 1997

I have often prided myself on being objective, but I'm not sure others are persuaded of this nor am I always convinced myself.

How do we measure our objectivity? A psychological study may call me an extrovert, making decisions on the basis of facts, not feelings. But I succumb to feelings — in fact, I'm often not courageous when I should be. Even my husband, who faced problems much more bravely than I, was frequently called a "softie."

Wasn't there a day when a front-page newspaper story didn't dare reveal an opinion? I can recall a feeling of disapproval at even a hint of bias or editorializing. Somebody once taught me that, but that day is gone. Students find an assignment difficult if they are told to write just what they see in a tree or a sky, instead of what it seems or might be or what they wish it would be. A court case can seem ridiculous when the jury is instructed not to consider anything but immediate facts or evidence. On the other hand, we appreciate a scientist who doesn't allow a feeling or whim to affect his research.

I am firm — even tough — with my children and grandchildren and the school children I love so much.

I don't want to be doting and ruin them. But those claims disappear in a hurry if their faults rise up and they need support and encouragement. I feel a fierce proprietorship in them and I want to defend them.

So I am weak and I want to be strong. What to do?

There is one example of objectivity that will never change. He is the God of truth, our Rock. This is a great hope to me. It keeps me from slipping and sliding around between opinions. Even the hymns where He is the sole object of our praise are the choicest. If I cherish this hope and use every opportunity to pass it on to grandchildren and students, I can keep a single eye and doting will subside.

Jean Belz

Pet Anecdotes

January-February 1998

The late afternoon was dark and gloomy with fog settling in. I looked out to see Mrs. Cardinal huddled and forlorn at the bird feeder. She lives next door with her mate who always looks brilliant and bold in his red attire no matter the weather. I could just imagine he might have said to her (who knows whether out of consideration or guilt?), "Dear, you really should get out for awhile before supper. I'll take care of things here while you wing it to the feeder." And I think I know, from my own experience, that now she wanted nothing more than to be home again.

I'm not one to attach human qualities to our furred or feathered friends, but much of the pleasure in them comes from seeing our behavior reflected in their antics. When our good friend arrived home from church one day and his dog jumped all over him, he grumbled, "Get down. Can't you see I've got my good clothes on?" To our friend's chagrin, he was to hear that story told and retold over the years.

Someone put cream in the cat's pan. When the only cat around the farmhouse where we lived suddenly rounded up many cats, my husband remarked that she probably had gone next door and exclaimed, "Come on up. They're serving cream at the neighbors." That same man once said to the dog next door, a new mother, "Susie, when are we going to get to see those pups of yours?" and Susie went home, carried each pup back to him, and laid it at his feet. Most unforgettable is the day the children in the neighborhood watched Butch, one more time, chase a passing truck. This time it was fatal, but his philosophical little mistress muttered, "That'll teach him a lesson."

Sure it's a dog's life, but sometimes things look up. When we dropped our grandmother off at the door of the school, seconds later, as we drove away, we looked again and there sat big old Abby beside the driver, eyes straight ahead, happy as a dog could be, and looking almost as perky as Grandma.

These tales are easily topped, but — they are simple pleasures, and the Lord God gave them all.

Jean Belz

Friendship in perspective

March-April 1998

When I was a little girl, my mother reminded me from time to time not to fret about having a close friend. She said it was better not to be dependent on one person nor to feel the necessity of checking with one person before I made choices or decisions. And I sensed that her advice was good. Perhaps this came from a desire for freedom — or even from a kind of pride.

But this philosophy had nothing to do with my mother's selfless kindness to others. I remember her staunch defense of a neighbor with a new baby when the husband and father railed at the baby's crying. She welcomed a little girl to our houseful of children when the mother — with only two daughters — suffered a headache. How many headaches must have plagued our mother? She regularly fed the tramps from the railroad hot bacon sandwiches and steaming coffee, mouth-watering to us children. She took in a very dirty boy from the neighborhood, scrubbed him top to toe, and sent him off in clean clothes.

Mother counseled the elderly widow next door in her bitter loneliness. She cautioned us and our high school friends concerning our studies, in fact, our very lives, and she congratulated us all in our successes. She wrote letters, shared books, and played piano duets with us. She welcomed us when we came in the door.

And yet she seemed to keep a part of herself to herself. She didn't live to enjoy friends in her old age. And I think that she gave more than she received. In contrast to my mother, I feel that instead of serving I have been served. I remember, as a child, learning what it meant to belong to a "mutual admiration society." How much better to befriend the one whom God puts in our way.

But the subject is too big. Who can define the dozens of kinds of friendships we hear or read about, some very shallow, some very deep? We suffer when a friend disappoints us, and we rejoice when he supports us. Do we make our own rules? Oftentimes.

If we live out our three score years and ten, we can reflect on crises that brought acquaintances that resulted in friendships that left rich memories. What a joy to shake a hand and hear, "Do you remember . . . ?" or "We knew you when . . . " Is there anything better? Only in the Scriptures. There the definition of a friend transcends all others.

JEAN BELZ

SUMMER STEPS

May-June 1998

The summer days are melting away. As I enjoy a pastry, sent by a friend, and a cup of coffee, what happier privilege than to decide whether to be summary or summery. The season has won. I can sum things up next time.

As I waited my turn at the gas pump on a fine, sunny morning, I was captivated by the family next door. While the young husband, dressed in shorts, washed his car outside the neatly fenced-in lawn, the dog played around the car, asking for and happily receiving a flick of the hose from time to time. Soon the screen door of the house opened and out popped a two-year-old, dressed for play. Immediately he ran up to the fence and had his turn at a quick spray. In no time, the attractive young mother tripped out with a swing, carefully set it down, and soon appeared with the baby and deposited him in the swing. Only then did she step over to the fence, and after she had chatted with her husband a moment and turned back to the baby, a brief little mist followed her.

There was no angry response or mean burst of water. Only a quick smile and a chuckle. How desirable it is for a wife to allow herself to be cultivated in such a way by her husband and for him to be confident and gentle in his love. And we can abide in Christ in the same way.

Jean Belz

Women

July-August 1998

Why is it so easy for me to say *coreopsis*? As I looked at the bright yellow bloom that bears the name, I realized it was very familiar to me — both its name and its beauty. And I know quite a few others. My mother taught them to me — always the botanical names. But my father tended the garden.

At the risk of worrying a well-worn subject, I'm compelled to say we women are a complicated lot. I despair of us, but I admire us. We say too much and sometimes stridently. But we are capable of storing innumerable things in our minds and hearts, and we can offer wisdom and love and ideas and comfort.

Some women seem hopelessly helpless, and yet they are loved. Others are towers of strength. Sometimes we can laugh at ourselves. Sometimes it is very hard. We puzzle ourselves. We want someone to tell us what we are thinking when we don't know ourselves. We can be terribly efficient, knowing what everyone in the household is or should be doing and, at the same time, doing a mountain of work ourselves. And, as my husband often observed, we can be sick and well at the same time.

And some of us are positively ingenious. Consider a woman's art in preparing a meal — arranging an inviting table, planning the menu, handling the ingredients, balancing the time for each dish, summoning the family, checking the hand-scrubbing, guiding the serving, and tempering the conversation.

Now think of a sewing machine. That same woman may not be mechanically minded, but she can take the machine apart and put it back together, oil it from top to bottom, thread the bobbin, thread the needle, adjust the tension, hold the material just right, and lo, a garment. I can't help thinking we fly blind oftentimes, but the Lord gives heavenly wisdom. And he allows names like spirea, rudbekia, viburnum, and scabiosa to roll off our tongues.

But you say, "You're living in the past. How often does a woman prepare a meal or sit down to sew nowadays? We have come a long way." Well, even if she is flying 35,000 feet above the Atlantic or handling a computer in San Francisco in the morning and keeping an appointment in New York City that night, she still must examine herself to see where she stands before a living God.

I treasure all these years of being a daughter, a young wife, a mother, a grandmother, and a great grandmother.

> *". . . but a woman who fears the Lord is to be praised. Give her the reward she has earned, and let her works bring her praise at the city gate."*
>
> – Proverbs 31:30-31

Jean Belz

All three are gifts from God

September-October 1998

One of the younger children was desperately concerned about the approaching school program. A schoolmate couldn't keep the pitch, and it was almost more than he could bear. His perfection in pitch was not matched by his perfection in patience.

Sure enough, during the presentation, our young friend's dismay mounted as his classmate happily sang, perhaps a little off key, until finally he reached forward to touch her elbow in an effort to quiet her. I feared he would embarrass the whole school. Just in time, a girl, a wee bit older, with a gentle but firm grasp kindly removed the young critic's hand from the arm of the offending little miss. The crisis was past and the Lord had used all sorts of gifts in a demonstration almost as effective as the performance itself.

How important it is to have folks who do things well, who have a sharp sense of the way things should be, and who expect it of others. But how cheering it is to know folks who go ahead enjoying life even if they are not experts or virtuosos. And best of all, how comforting to have mediators who display moderation and wisdom when we need it most.

Listen to your grandkids' music

November-December 1998

Some years ago I thought there would be no problem in planning an automobile trip with two or three grandchildren a season, ultimately including them all. Not so easy. Heart ailment, summer jobs, conflicts of all kinds, even old age crept in. Those who did go in their high school years remember the miles covered in the Northwest and the Northeast happily, as do I, but, surprising to me, a little hazily.

In spite of a dwindling memory, I recall vividly every stop and host, besides myriad details. Of course, for the youngsters, ten or fifteen years of college, jobs, marriage, and children have intervened to blur the few weeks we spent together gazing at the peaks of the Canadian Rockies, thrilling at the sight of the Pacific, the St. Lawrence River, New York City, or fluffy white clouds in an incredibly blue sky over Nebraska. I have had many hours to review, in my mind and heart, the sights, reunions, hospitality, discussions and even mishaps along the way. And as one of the fathers still says of the venture, "It helped shaped them."

This year, after a gap of at least ten years, I did it again — this time with a sixteen-year-old grandson.

There was everything to be apprehensive about — a boy with an almost new driver's license, a car certainly not new, winter time, weather, roads, schedules, and, not the least, my nervous system. But they all held.

Try it. Talk. Listen to one another's music. Pray. Go over family background. Serve snacks. Study the map. Choose stops. Be positive. Be hopeful. Have you ever driven all day and, as the sun is beginning to drop, turned just the right corner onto just the right street and found just the right house where supper is ready and a loving family is welcoming you? The Lord did it all.

Team Spirit

January-February 1999

A day or two ago, several of us made an assault on the library workroom. Five women sorted and shelved hundreds of books waiting to be accessioned. We filled many boxes with magazines and papers for recycling and sorted others into categories. We moved visual aid equipment and carried out everything we thought didn't belong there. You can be sure, among those women, there were five strong opinions. We discovered some other strong opinions when some of the items were carried back in. We dusted and vacuumed and cleared tabletops and desks. It is quite a new room. It looked beautiful when we finished. We were dead tired. So tired that I have to use short sentences to tell about it. No one person could have done it alone that afternoon.

But the best part about it was working with the other women, all different in personality but no one excluding the preferences of the others. The one in charge, after recovering from the initial shock of seeing so much help barge in, quickly took over so that the rest of us knew what to do. One of the women seems to be a compulsive organizer and space saver. Before we knew it, she had found new space and shoved something into it that just fit. Another younger friend was merciless in discarding outdated stuff, but once in a while she would find something so wonderfully old that she fervently guarded it. Still another hoarded a dozen or so books in a little box to "take home and read." Finally, our last friend, working hard in the religion section, made some firm decisions. If one of us expressed strong disapproval of an author's theology or his influence in any other way, she would say, "Well, we don't need that!" It was exhilarating and exhausting.

The temptations are terrible. Most of the books beg to be read or, at least, scanned. To read them all would be an education, but we aren't up to that in this age of distillation. Francis Bacon says that only a few books are to be chewed and digested. May the Lord give us grace to choose wisely.

Beautiful Land

March-April 1999

Why do I think the Iowa landscape is so beautiful? Someone might say, "Because it is." But someone else says, "I'm sure I don't know."

I sat in a schoolroom recently and looked out a bare window at the brown winter fields where one slope met another against the gray horizon. To the left in the foreground was a leafless tree with a tiny evergreen nearby. There seemed to be no attempt at artistry. But I sat there drinking it in.

I have just come from the seashore in the Southeast, watching the endless sky and water and marveling at the power and mystery of the tides. The highways had gradually let us down to sea level so that we scarcely noticed it. Then it was flat country and we were surrounded by trees. Where was the horizon?

All the way home trees and flowers were full and lush. As we drove through the Smokies and the southern states, there was a parade of dogwood and redbud in the timber along the highways. The trees, in full bloom, seemed to dance along trying to keep up with us. I wonder that we manage to keep going in Iowa without dogwood. But I guess we fall back on wild plum, that appears in whitish clouds along the fence rows, and on every shade of purple lilac.

But aren't the prairie states, say Illinois and Iowa, all alike? Not quite. Iowa is a rolling land divided into tufted fields like a quilt and cut through with rivers, these flowing into the Mississippi and those into the Missouri. The familiarity of it all is the secret, I think. On this same trip I heard a man quoted as having told his children, "Home is where you are." How good the Lord is to have put this longing and this satisfaction in our hearts.

Anticipate one of life's thrills

May-June 1999

You never know when a happy experience is coming your way. It is easy to turn it down and miss out. But the Lord knows.

Many years ago, at least fifty if not sixty, a young man came to our door on a warm evening in the fall just as darkness was gathering. He did not explain much at all, but we quickly understood that help was badly needed in his home around the corner about a half mile away. He was hurrying into town to get the doctor. A baby was coming!

We immediately began to put the job onto one another. I thought my mother-in-law should go because she was older and wiser. She thought I should go because I was younger and had more children. We both thought my sister should go because she was a nurse. My sister and I went — loaded down with enough clothes and supplies for ten babies.

There was silence in the barnyard as we drove in. Inside, a little girl looked at us gravely from a high chair while a small boy slept the evening away. As the young mother lay on the bed, my sister quickly did all she could to prepare her for the struggle. With absolutely no understanding or purpose, I kindled the fire in the kitchen cookstove and put a big kettle of water on to boil.

At last we could see the lights of the car in the driveway. It seemed to us the doctor would never come into the house — till finally my sister called, "Tell the doctor to come! This baby's head is popping in and out!" He did come and the baby was born-a beautiful little girl. We would love to have taken the credit, but it was very nice to give the doctor the responsibility, and God above was in complete charge. The doctor was scathing over the amount of water I was boiling and ordered a very small amount instead. When he called out, "Who wants the baby?" I dashed to the bedroom and shouted, "I do." My sister said later that she knew I would come running. It was my indescribable privilege to clean the baby up and clothe her while our nurse helped the doctor take care of the mother and then made her comfortable in a fresh bed. She looked lovely lying there. Our joy knew no bounds.

We have guarded that marvelous evening in our memories ever since. A few years ago when a group of women came to my home, I asked if any of them knew the young mother, whom I named. The woman herself, now a grandmother, stepped forward and we recalled the evening together. What if we had let someone else go that night?

How rich the Lord is toward us!

Order my steps

July-August 1999

When I considered my feet, for a moment I thought, "They don't seem so old — maybe even a little youthful" — and then I knew I was wrong. They are old. But where have they been? What have they done? A flood of memories swept over me.

My sisters and I ran down the alley, climbed two fences, struggled through a bed of nettles, and crossed the railroad track to get to the little town park in time for a picnic and baseball game. We hiked to a farm two miles from town and walked out of town on the railroad track with no fear of danger. We toiled up the hill, lugging groceries from the grocery store to our home. We pedaled bicycles tirelessly at every opportunity. We tramped rugged hills on outings and trudged through state and county fairs. We delivered newspapers to customers' homes. I recall complaining about hurting feet, but I do not remember ever thanking God for them.

Away at college I walked long city blocks to classes and several times long distances across the city to attend concerts. When I had small children, the trips up and down stairs were countless. So were those to the garden and to the clothesline. Even so, the entire family would sometimes stumble over the winter cornfields and hike on up the road to visit friends. We walk impossible distances and stand for interminable hours, and we are ready to go again. We walk across the room or across the lawn, not giving a thought to the wonder of it, the provision for it.

Just when I think I can't go another step, I see that I have gone from there to here. When I can't do that, it will be all right. Tired feet don't matter. Thankful hearts do.

Never stop singing!

September-October 1999

As a child, I did not learn the Scriptures, but my father and I sang hymns together, he the melody, I the alto, as I struggled at the piano. I think I thought he was quite an old man when, in truth, he was only in his late forties. "I Need Thee Every Hour" was our best with some German hymns not far behind.

What good did it do when I didn't even know what we were singing about? Untold good. But I'll tell a little. I learned to honor hymn singing, to want more, to hear the parts, and to nurture a little of the longing for peace and joy that it brought.

Parents frequently say concerning their budding pianists, "I don't really care how far he goes, if he just learns to play hymns." Well, if he can play hymns, he has come a long way. Play the right notes, keep up the tempo, bring your hands down together, watch the time, give each note its full value, follow the words.

But you don't need a piano to sing. Probably one of the happiest customs that came about in our home was singing a hymn before breakfast and before supper. We went through a number of hymn books over the years when our children were growing up. What a delight it was when I realized we were singing "While Shepherds

Watched Their Flocks" to Handel's music-in four parts. We were on our way. We cheerfully endured the changing of the boys' voices because they were soon holding their own and offering great harmony. No one in the family was a virtuoso. That was a small matter. We sang one hymn for a week. By the end of the week most of us knew the entire hymn, and at the end of thirty or forty years most of us still know them.

And the advantage was with us — that is, God's goodness was upon us. Not just our children sang, but everyone who came near sang — guests, workers, grandchildren, and school children. My husband loved to tell about a successful schoolmaster in Germany. His rule was to "teach the children, care for them, and sing all the time." One of the memories I treasure most is going into the chapel on a cloudy, lonely Sunday afternoon and finding two boarding boys at the piano. They were going through the hymnal to find all the hymns they had learned during their stay at the school. What enthusiasm, what encouragement. To take part in honoring the God in heaven in this way, to exalt Christ, and to understand the Christian experience is His unspeakable gift.

Girls

November-December 1999

So many significant years have passed since I wrote about boys, I realize that I was feeling a little defensive about girls. How easily we are affected by what we read and hear. I discovered that a generation of thought and opinion regarding the position and rights of women had almost penetrated my own tough stance. At least, I thought it was tough.

But, thanks be to God, the joy and privilege of being a woman rose up in my heart, and I want to mention some of the things that make girls such treasures.

When a baby girl enters the home, immediately you can see all the pleasures and comforts she can bring to those around her. Count on it. Tell her so, even when she seems too young to understand. A baby girl is beautiful, and she is lovely in her sweet little clothes.

Even when she is older and, insisting on dressing herself, she puts her clothes on backwards or cuts a lock out of her hair, she is irresistible. You don't know where you might find a safety pin holding something together or a smear of lipstick blissfully applied. As she begins to prefer five-year-old friends to family members now and then, you may feel a twinge of loss, but hang on.

Soon she is approaching her tenth year. She can make brownies and set the table, she has some strong opinions about what she wants to wear, she has her classmates pretty well figured out, but, best of all, she has a conscience, and she is strongly aware of who the Lord is and of the importance of the Scriptures. A friend once called one of our daughters, at this age, "blithe spirit." How cheerful! How encouraging! All this time, the curve of her cheek is becoming prettier, her hair shinier, and her gifts are becoming more apparent. Are you saying, "Yes, and so are her faults"? Of course they are, but stay in charge. Give her every wholesome opportunity possible, help her appreciate her brothers and sisters, teach her, by assignment and example, to serve others, have a ban in the home on pouting, and don't quarrel. Anything less than this high view of femininity, with all the joy that it entails, is demeaning and robs the family of some of its greatest blessings.

If you are looking for a reward, you will get one. The sister who endured her brothers' teasing will have their respect and love, you will have her respect and love, and she will be a ready servant, eager to please the Lord.

Families

January-February 2000

We were talking about families' relationships with each other. How far should we go in entering into another family's life? Do we want someone else to influence our children so that their influence goes beyond our own? Not ordinarily. Our children need to know that they can find love and counsel with us. But when they do, they can understand better the love and counsel of others. Isn't this a touchy subject? When I look back over the years, I recall stressful, tense times when other adults did not want our advice for their children, nor did we for ours.

One of the best rules to go by is to teach respect for the children's elders. We can do this by respecting them ourselves and avoiding criticism of each other and of adult friends–yes, and of the children, too. A good way to establish this habit is to speak words of kindness and encouragement when the matter arises. A young boy complained a little bit about his mother's inviting another boy, who was away from home, in for breakfast so often, but she has just gone cheerfully ahead, enjoying the hospitality she offers and setting a great example of kindness and love.

Another rule is never to drive a wedge between parent and child. My husband often said he would like a sign over the entrance to the campus saying: Honor thy father and mother. It would solve a multitude of problems. It's God's word! There are so many opportunities to say, "Well, of course, if your parents won't do this for you, we will." Not good.

Does this mean that I never want any help from anyone? Not at all. When my older children were very small, loving, wise friends took them over so that my husband and I could work with the church choir. Those years brought great blessing and spiritual profit. Those friends are still loving friends. As our children grew up, we were happy that they had trusted Sunday school and day school teachers. What a privilege. When the time came for them to go off to college, we could not hold them any longer, nor would we have tried to. My husband told several college professors we were putting the youngsters under their care, and we counted on them to train them in the best ways. And they did, through thick and through thin. The fellowship of believers is unsurpassed. As we build one another up and welcome the gifts we have for one another, we have riches.

Perspective on those kids

March-April 2000

Has everything been discussed? Hardly. In the face of beauty all around, it is tempting to revel in the delights of the June sky, the deep shades of peonies, the bright lilies, the luscious strawberries, and the beautiful greens in the trees, shrubs, and lawns, but something more tender keeps coming to mind.

When I claim to be objective in my views of my children and my grandchildren, I'm pretty sure to hear some scoffing in the background– at least a chuckle. And why not have some prejudice? If I can't be supportive of a son or a daughter, who will be?

We probably know our own children better than anyone else does. We can allow for weaknesses and strengths of character.

How indulgent should we be? Do we require more of others than of ourselves? Are we able to be apart from our children from time to time? If someone else disciplines the child, do we erase the effect by sympathizing over much with him? Do we rejoice with our children in their desire and efforts to be independent? Do we prepare them for this? Do we set them free?

On the other hand, if we know a teaching or habit is

good, do we have the courage to instill it in the mind of the child? I've noticed that when the courage is lacking, the child's character is weakened, and the parents' excuses set in.

How refreshing it is when in spite of– or because of– our fierce, intense love for our children, we can stand at a great enough distance to see them as God's children who must first serve Him. The smothering heaviness is removed, and a desirable family emerges.

Enjoy it

May-June 2000

It is hard for me to throw off fretting and worry when the schedule gets too full or my hopes and plans don't seem to be working out. But the relief and deliverance that the Lord gives is beyond our understanding. Comfort and wonder come in little things that take away the burden.

I planted a butterfly bush. Somehow I thought its blooms would resemble butterflies, but instead, as I came up the walk, a beautiful monarch was lighting on the deep purple bloom. A little later a deep red cardinal suddenly took my attention in the garden. He was poised on a post, and I thought it wasn't like him, when, all at once, he was pecking away at a wonderfully full sunflower. As I stepped out the door into the early evening, hundreds of fireflies silently appeared here and there and then vanished. The lilies — day, Asiatic, Oriental, tiger — have been on parade all summer and now there is no greater pleasure than having a ten-year-old run to the flower bed that she planted and bring in a bunch of pink and white cosmos for a centerpiece.

Joy comes with visitors, old friends and new, young and old, with a youngster sitting at the piano, with a little girl rolling her eyes and putting her tongue in her cheek exactly like a cousin before her, with a boy learning to drive a truck and to lift heavy things. It comes with a girl, or a boy, dashing off with her father to a grown-up meeting. It comes via e-mail with the news of a new job for someone you love. It comes with the high approval of an uncle for his niece as he observed her on her job all summer. Joy comes with a meeting of the minds during a prayer meeting, with a strong response to a solid sermon, with an understanding of another's suffering. It is deep and full of meaning. Joy comes with a laying aside of petty matters and giving worries over to the Lord just as He has told us we must do.

Jesus, keep them near the cross

September-October 2000

Not long ago I sat behind a young couple during a church service. The youngest of their three small children lay in his seat sleeping the sleep of a baby quite new to this world. Finally after lying quietly during much singing and some speaking, his tight shut eyes slowly opened and he began to look around, seeing yet not seeing. While the worshipers sang full, exuberant harmonies, the baby stretched and moved his head as if to hear more. "What's this?" he seemed to wonder. He twisted his mouth blissfully, and then nestled back into sleepytown. What more could we ask for our children? Is there something better for them to wake up to? I was reminded of a family member who read the Scriptures aloud beside his son in his crib. That time will never come again for a parent, and the privilege is precious.

There is a way of life where noise and hurts prevail. One shout follows another and each is in mean, accusing tones. Insults and sarcasm are the conversation norm. Entertainment centers blare meaningless talk and music–even worse, destructive talk and music.

I love the memory of hearing vibrant gospel hymns in the home of friends as we prepared for Sunday morning breakfast and the worship service to follow. When the custom of singing *Messiah* together on a Sunday afternoon developed, deep, quiet joy in a new realization of the power of the Scriptures became ours for life. As the children filled the hours with piano practice, a discipline in the household was put firmly in place. The sight of a class of fourth through sixth graders reading along silently at their desks as their teacher reads aloud is inspiring, especially when it is contrasted with rowdier behavior in their free moments.

We may ask, "But what is the use of it all? We may struggle to maintain dignity and calm in our homes and then see it destroyed in the face of public uproar. The confidence and quiet we establish in our homes will almost be overshadowed by the lack of it outside. Singing to our babies, holding firmly to the youngsters in their growing up years, urging our teenagers on to responsibilities and to the trustworthiness of the God in heaven will surely be for naught as forces of evil seem to take over our lives."

Well, no one can take an inner calm away from us. Or a quiet spirit. Or the experience of praying. Or the sweet influences of hymns. Let us practice all these blessings in our lives.

Receiving with grace

November-December 2000

Oh, the pain and joy of growing up -- the worries and fears of those years and the comfort and bliss. I remember looking at much admired teenagers when I was quite small and wondering how my legs would hold me at such a height when I was that big! On the other hand, everything around me was a challenge, and I felt as if I could handle it all. As I grew up into more self-conscious years, I realized there were quite a few things I couldn't handle.

Through most of the years, my teachers held untold interest for me. I wanted to learn from them, know what they did, do what they did. Now I know that great air of mystery between them and me amounted to almost nothing, that they were people, too.

One late winter afternoon, my mother sent me on an errand to the home of a friend who was the landlady of two of my favorite teachers. The friend invited me in to her dining room, pretty and warm. There were my teachers! They were sitting calmly at the table, eating cake and drinking coffee. Our friend smilingly invited me to sit down and have some too, and the teachers also smiled, in the most friendly manner. The cake, they said, was white cake with black walnuts–my favorite. It didn't seem to be a problem for them to include me.

But it was too much. At that age I had some social graces, but not enough to sit down and make such a dream come true. I declined and went home. Upon my arriving home, my mother, as was her custom, asked me for details concerning the errand, and when I told her that I did not accept the cake, she said, "But, why not?" And I thought, "Yes, why not?" And I have thought that many times since.

I learned from that afternoon's experience. First, to enjoy good food when it is offered, and not hesitate to invite someone, even a lowly school child, to sit at my table if I have something he might enjoy. Make it as easy as possible for him. Second, and more important, learn grace. Be gracious. Give and expect no return. Receive and do not expect to pay back. Rejoice.

> *Oh, taste and see that the Lord is good. Come buy wine and buy milk, without money and without price.*

Founders' Perspective

January-February 2001

What did we want for our children? Were we so purposeful, even in our marriage? It doesn't seem so now. But we took it all seriously. We had great respect for one another, never dreaming of being unfaithful in any way, of any betrayal, and that lasted throughout our lives together. We worked very hard, we were careful in money matters, and we were conscientious in church responsibilities. We were strict in disciplining our children. But the delight did not come with all that.

Whether because of our rigorous lifestyle or in spite of it, a whole new way of thinking and living descended on us, or was thrust upon us, as we realized who the Lord Jesus Christ was and what kind of God we were actually serving. And we were delighted.

The children looked different to us, our lives together appeared abundant and running over with blessings. There seemed no end of possibilities for us all, not in a material way, but in learning more in every area: reading, music, speaking, writing, and in understanding of God's world and his people. Most of all, the opportunity lay in serving God in the name of Christ. To educate the children ourselves, that is, to have them under our direction with the help of godly teachers, became all important, and it has paid off.

We have not given them everything, but they learned to think for themselves, or better, to think God's thoughts after Him. Without ordinary distractions they were forced to be creative — living simply. We hoped for this same way of life for many children who came under our guidance and protection.

Their lives are not simple now. They are doing complicated and demanding things. They are surely better fitted for what they are doing if they have their chins up and a single eye for the Lord.

Kindness: not effortless

March-April 2001

Thirty years ago, my granddaughter made a sampler for me with two words simply worked into the fabric — "Kindness helps." What a nice, easy word. How harmless. What simpler character trait to come by. And it is even part of the fruit of the Spirit!

We might begin to think that this part of our Christian growth, our godliness, is effortless.

It does seem as if some are born to be kind. Let's hope that their manner offsets that of some of the rest of us. But we can't rest on that. What great examples some are, saying just the right thing at the right time, performing a comforting task in the most fitting way, smiling just when we need it most, encouraging us when all around are disparaging or even defaming in what they say. We will do well to follow their example.

But how can we be kind without indulging folks in their mistakes or in their oafish manner? Perhaps the kindest thing we can do is give them a word of caution, but the Lord knows their hearts and ours, and vengeance belongs to Him, not us. I want to hold my tongue and step back when I am inclined to step in and take over, but, on the other hand, I need to make a conscious effort to show kindness — not just play defense.

And this is a problem. I am too lazy. Or I want this for myself. I don't want to give it away. I might miss out on something better if I take time for this person. Or if I am too kind, I'll be too transparent. I won't have anything in reserve. Silly excuses? Of course, and the Lord is well able to banish them all. How kind He is to allow us to take on His attribute in our homes, in our schools and churches, in our neighborhoods, and among those we have been despising.

Clothesline

May-June 2001

"The men are fixing the clothesline!" Happy news! The post had been bumped several months earlier, and the lines were loose. Anything hung on them made a dismal sight. Now they were straight and tight, a lovely sight. Who cares about a clothesline anyway? Well, I do. During the rolling blackouts in California in the spring, I heard a discussion on the air about the possibility of hanging clothes outside on a clothesline. There was some approval, but such an idea was far removed from most people's thinking. It just wouldn't do in most neighborhoods, and I suppose I might agree. Still, I don't want the privilege taken from me.

Some months ago, my neighbor ran into a problem. She is a young wife and mother and always eager to learn some new thing about homemaking. But just now her dryer wouldn't work. What to do? I suggested hanging her clothes outside. "Oh," she said, as much as to say, "Can you do that?" A little later there was her laundry draped over the outdoor lines, sans clothespins. Why would you need clothespins in a dryer? I think I lent her some and, soon after, bought her a starter package. She was soon in business for herself, and now her clothes hang neatly, looking colorful and fresh in the breeze.

It wasn't always easy. As a child, my sisters and I braved the elements to hang everything outside that we could, enduring frozen fingers and then stumbling back into the house with garments stiff as boards and needing to finish drying next to the heating stove. As a young wife in a rural community, I remarked to a friend one day that I did not know how I would dry my clothes when winter came. She answered heartily, "Oh, you'll hang them in the living room like the rest of us do." I determined that I would not, but did I? The years seem far away. Our mother taught us to make sure the clothes were dry, then dampen them for ironing, and iron them carefully. If starching was necessary, we did it. How many socks and washcloths have I hung on a line? A countless number.

Was it all worth it? You could say we didn't know any better. But we read books, enjoyed music and good conversation, and, yes, we actually had laundry days so that the job was finished, and we could take it up another day. Not long ago a friend from my era walked past the clothesline and said, "I love to look at your laundry on the line — pretty pastels hung so nicely." And then I was privileged to bring it into the house, fold it, and put it away. Luxury? There is nothing like it. One of the Lord's simple pleasures. Which ones do you have?

Cluttery, wonderful boys

July-August 2001

Those boys! Just when I thought they did a fine job on their rooms, they walked out the door leaving important school papers behind. And they left the door open on this chilly morning! What shall I do? Well, not what I often did in former years — when our own boys were rushing from comfy beds to meals to jobs to classes to the soccer field and back again. I am sure I often despaired, raised my voice, threatened dire punishment, allowed my blood pressure to rise, and slumped in a chair when they were all gone. And when those boys were gone — and often longed for — more school boys took their places and suffered the same treatment.

Of course, I am not throwing out all discipline and training. If we don't guide them, who will? Some boys arrive with tidy habits, but I often say nothing but a good wife will teach the others. The untidy ones look right at their own clothes and don't recognize them, love a dry towel but never think of hanging up the wet one, revel in a few moments to enjoy a soda or a bowl of hot noodles. They don't really want me to come near, but they really need me. My job is to swallow hard, brace my shoulders, thicken my skin, and go in and help them. I am persuaded that we are in this together.

But you ask, "Why are you even dealing with those boys? I thought your day was past." So did I, but this fall when we happily needed more space, it fell to my lot to care for five boys. It is a joy. The boys are lovable, kind, respectful, helpless and helpful at the same time, and cluttery. I am not unaware of possible subterfuge, but I cannot be constantly suspicious or nagging. Praise God for this opportunity to serve Him in a new and old way.

When every minute counts

September-October 2001

I have no greater joy than the quiet thrill of walking the length of our classroom building and getting a glimpse of the teaching and learning taking place in the various rooms. As I glance around the biology room, I often think, "I could have been a biologist. After all, I am alive, and all these pictures and diagrams are part of all of us and the world around us." But there is more to it than that, and I am lacking in dedication. Just now the algebra class is crowding in, clamoring for their test grades and full of questions for a patient teacher. One math teacher is planning to take a group of students to a math competition! The art room beckons with its painty odors and pleasant clutter. Just a look around reveals talent among students we hadn't guessed was there.

I love the quiet order of the library — even its lack of technical advantage can't detract from shelves of good reading and resources. Look at the rows of books, the tables and chairs, the sun streaming in through the sky lights, the students hard at their assignments. It's beautiful. The workroom next door has a wonderful disorder — delightful and encouraging to me.

Across the hall the deep, confident tones of the voice

Jean grew up in the family of a German immigrant meat merchant, her father Paul Franzenburg

Jean was the oldest of four girls, and with four older siblings, born and raised in northwest Iowa, mostly in the town of Pierson. Jean graduated from high school in Conrad, where she met Max Belz. They married, they both became Christians, he entered the pastorate, and they started the church at Cono (right) in 1948. Max and Jean (below) with Joel, Mark and Julie.

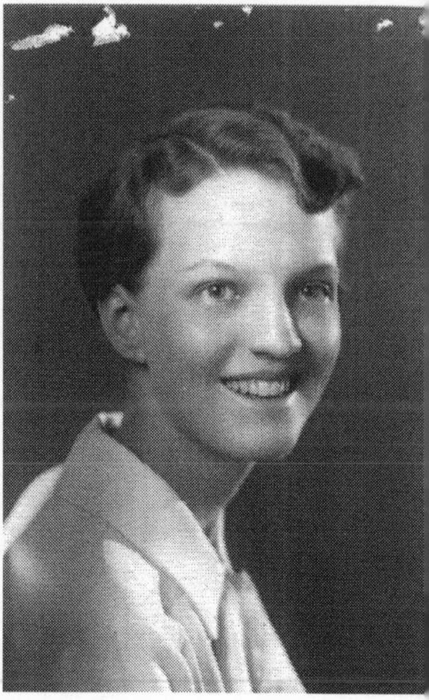

Max and Jean Belz were married 41 years before cancer took Max's life in 1978. She would continue to live on the Cono campus, accompanying the choir, teaching literature and Latin and always making the most of gardens and flower beds.

The Belzes did a lot of child rearing in one end of a 70-ft. Quonset-shaped building which also served as church, printshop and fellowship hall. The Cono school was founded in 1951; boarding students came in 1960 — and so the family, church, and school operation grew.

By comparison to much of American life surrounding it, life was hard in 1950s rural Iowa, and celebrations like this, offered by the church family, were rare. The sign below, ubiquitous on the Cono campus for many years, accurately described a Cono priority.

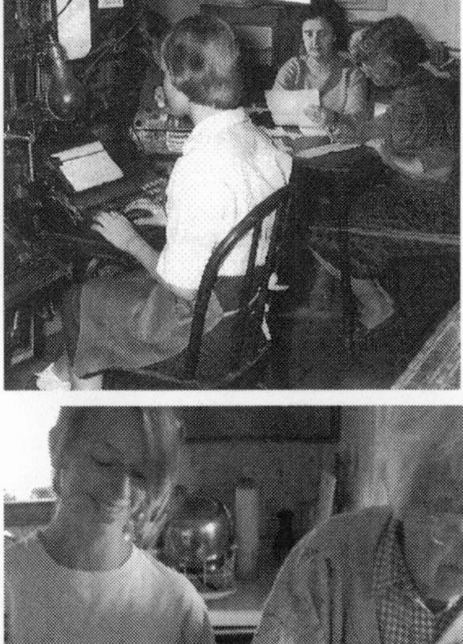

Proofreading, teaching Latin and English, and housing boarding students well into her eighties, Jean also accompanied choirs and loved watching Cono sports teams perform.

Among her many avocations, Jean loved little more than gardening, and she enjoyed plenty of it in the rich Iowa soil. Meanwhile, many students learned to cook under her tutelage.

With extended family around the country and across the ocean, Jean kept her house at Cono as a place for family meals and reunions. She also kept dorm children in her house until she was 85 years old. In the kitchen and dining room she continued to read, write, and entertain guests until her death in 2010 at 91.

Less than two months before her death in September 2010, three sisters, eight children, their spouses, and most of her 31 grandchildren and 31 great grandchildren gathered during a final family reunion.

of the doctrine teacher assure me that our students are not going out into the world untaught. Almost invariably they enter school unsure of themselves and what they believe, and they reach the end with a solid view of who God is and what their relationship to Him is. I can hear junior high students laughing and talking excitedly as they match wits with their history teacher. The business manager comes out of his office solemnly. Is everything all right? But he smiles and we are encouraged.

As we pass the fourth-sixth grades, the youngsters are all bent over their desks as if they wouldn't think of doing anything else. Their teacher is just as quiet and busy. They learn to be meticulous in there. Great things are going on in the lower grades. One little boy has suddenly caught on to reading. Another, who reads very well, is standing in the corner. That happens. Each little girl is cuter than the last.

We wish we could barge into the principal's office and discuss a few things, but we enter cautiously and are encouraged in whatever pursuit is ours. Next there will be either a computer class going on, an English class, or one of several ESL classes. Across the hall there are the science classes carried on by a hard-working teacher usually appearing with his arms full of books or equipment. There are English classes and Bible classes all over the place — *Macbeth*, short stories,

American literature, and a deep study of world literature.

At the end of the hall is the secretary's office. Do you need the telephone, a lozenge, the copier, a wandering student? Ask her. And just beyond we hope to find the headmaster who may have just come from directing the choir, or is now directing the journalism class, or will be dealing with the maintenance man or the builders, or is taking a phone call from far away.

These teachers are sold out to the Lord and committed to teaching the children put in their way. The desire and opportunity do not really go away. I was working with a friend in the library, retired from teaching long ago. She said longingly, "When I walk down the hall, I just wish I were teaching again." And as she gazed off into the years gone by, she said, "I used to make them look up all the words they didn't know and write the meanings and learn how to spell them." And when I responded with some question, she didn't hear me. She was still gazing off as she said, "and proper names, too."

You have GOT to look

November-December 2001

Since the white shop and the temporary classroom building have been moved, for better purposes, there is nothing to obstruct my view of the evening sky. Now night after night, we see the colors gather and perform in such dramatic fashion we can't begin to convey their beauty in words. The afternoon may be hung with dark clouds and then, as evening approaches, a thin line of light appears on the horizon, and that begins to widen as lovely shades of pink, coral, purple, lavender, pale blue, and dark blue, too, take over the whole, wide west. Sometimes, the colors change their tints a wee bit and creep up to the north as if to say, "There is always more."

Sometimes the sun makes one last appearance in a perfect ball of fire, blazing orange as it rests for an instant on the horizon and then drops out of sight before we can think about it. As the moon waxes in her ladylike manner, there is nothing more graceful and lovely than her holding her place in the western sky only an hour or two after the sun sets. For years, I squeezed this spectacle in between buildings. Now the sky is the limit.

Some years ago a young friend on campus would call me and say, "Mrs. Belz, you have GOT to look out the window." Soon, our households tried not to let such splendor go by without reminding one another. I vowed then that I would always go to the window.

My husband often asked me to take a walk with him. I wish I had gone every time.

But he loved to bring home a weed or a flower or a rock or a bug and show us all the intricacies and beauty of the handiwork of our Creator. It is easy to become jaded where loveliness is concerned. We are indifferent, unimpressed. We are surfeited with pleasing sights all around. Our food is alluring, attractive clothing is obtainable, and homes are luxurious. Our children are bonny, and they are loaded with opportunities. Handsome books lie unread. The arts are all around.

This is a plea, of course, for each one of us to appreciate the incredible sights near us, ready to be absorbed and treasured. What have you enjoyed looking at today? A big red apple? A baby's cheek? An antique desk? A smiling teenager? An intriguing book? Be sure to go to the window.

Magnify the Lord with Me

January-February 2002

"... but they are not my primary carrier." That is all I have to say to get the attention of the receptionist or the person at the other end of the phone line. They have all the evidence — the color of my hair, the crackle in my voice, and the year indicated on the line for the date of my birth. But my intention is to hang in there. The temptation is to chuck the whole thing and never deal with an insurance company again. With or without insurance, I am surely a burden to somebody. But conventional wisdom says chucking's not practical, and we must make plans and save against a day of trouble. So I am reluctantly willing — and thankful. In fact, I am one who, upon paying the premium and then receiving the amount of the claim, feels that I have been given a gift. My grasp of it all doesn't run very deep.

You are probably thinking, "That woman needs help." But the fact is that life, through our Heavenly Father, is bringing me many joys, payments of many claims because of Christ. I could walk down the long hall this morning with a spring in my step; sometimes I can't; the news came of the birth of a healthy baby boy; a boy brought his Latin average up above passing; there is the prospect of snow in the air after many months without it; my children and grandchildren claim the love of Christ through trials and blessings; colleagues are supportive; our nation is free; we hear God's word presented as the truth. Forget the introspection and magnify the Lord with me.

Have Clean Shirt, Will Function

March-April 2002

There go the boys again, and they have changed their shirts. Why are they all wearing work shirts? Well, because they are particular about their clothes, and we expect them to work, so, of course, they are wearing work shirts. Just a little while ago they had their classroom shirts on, and we expected that. Those poor boys. Really? No.

Their parents have wonderfully supplied them with everything they need. In a plain sort of way they live in a kind of luxury.

But there is always that schedule — or sometimes that emergency. And the boys are expected to be flexible. It is their turn to work in the kitchen. They must carry out the trash. A truck just arrived to be unloaded. The cement truck is coming, and the forms aren't quite ready. Someone must finish mowing the soccer field before tomorrow's game. There is rain in the forecast. We oldsters want the snow off the walks by school time.

And this is what we hope for. We could build our school on a philosophy of doing the work for the youngsters — and our philosophy does include working alongside them — but we want a simple way of life that includes rough and ready training, so that means many shirts. There is a thrill that comes in seeing the boy shoulder the responsibility with no complaint and with a cheerful willingness. And the thrill returns when he appears in the library, ready for class, a neat shirt and pants that become him, thinking nothing of the restrictions he is under.

It is beyond believing how fast our boy can get out of his classroom shirt into his soccer jersey, but there he is, racing madly in cold and in heat. By supper time, he is back in his classroom shirt with hair slicked back (or sticking up straight). Perhaps there is a concert tonight. By 7:30 he stands coolly waiting to walk up to the platform in his white shirt and red tie.

And then it is Sunday morning, time for the worship service. I am suddenly aware of a row of boys in front of me, most of them wearing white shirts, some even snowy. I feel a quick tug in my heart. They do their own laundry. They live in snug quarters. The demands on their time seem endless. We expect them to be ready with just the right shirt for every situation. They come up smiling.

Power in weakness

May-June 2002

We aren't accustomed to striking out on Sunday afternoon, but a recital took us to town, and we were winding our way on the city streets bound for the concert hall. At an intersection, a young man waited and then, as we passed him, ran across from the neighborhood drugstore to the other side. He wore shorts and a loose white shirt and was carrying a floor fan. We were all feeling the first heat of summer in spite of the pleasant day. Suddenly, everything became drab, discouraging, almost without hope. Why did he buy a fan?

Where was he taking the fan? Was a parent sick, or a young brother or sister? Was he rooming with someone who was sick? Or were he and his roommate just hot in their room and sick of it all? Did he really have enough money for the fan? Perhaps someone gave him the money and said, "Go buy a fan." Maybe it cheered him to make the decision. Who was his roommate anyway? Was his mother somewhere wondering about his welfare and hoping he was spending his money and time well? Was he trying too much and was he too proud to say so? Would the fan solve the problem?

What do I need? Compassion and peace of mind, I am sure. I don't want to get into a position where I am desperate for a fan. But what if I do? I am not exempt from such suffering. I know a desolation that comes from bad news — sickness in the family, someone giving in to an addiction, failure of some kind in business, or disappointment in someone I love. But there is really no bad news. My weakness is God's opportunity to show me his power, his kindness, his love.

Freedom which your will appoints

July-August 2002

Enough about boys?! Never! But it is past time to talk again about my close favorite — girls. I think I left off with the joy and love that comes with seeing a daughter grow up, becoming desirable in every way, in the family, in the workaday world, and in her own family as she takes a husband and knows the inexpressible happiness of being a mother. I know this is not for every girl, and the Lord knows more about that than I do, but the discussion is profitable. Even on my way to my desk this morning a new book on this very subject was being touted on NPR.

But the pitfalls on the way! What shall we do? How do we stand ready to help? Take advantage of everything positive. Admire the smooth, curved cheek and the shiny hair. I started talking about shiny hair years ago — and my mother before me (eighty years!) — but it is no less beautiful now than then. Hold out for a fresh fragrance about your person and your daughter's — in body and in spirit. Steer the conversation into wholesome subjects — good books, sports, jobs to be done, friends and ways to help or enjoy them, learning to cook, shopping, listening to a sermon, plans for college, and then act on these things. Don't leave them there. Assume that your daughter or friend is listening, that it can be done, that she will join you in these ideas and will enjoy actively pursuing them. She is lovely, but she is a victim of the times and the culture, and she doesn't need to be. Be courageous and encourage her.

You may be thinking (you probably are) submission, submission, submission. That's right — that's where the happiness is. To God Himself and consequently to a marriage, to parents, to younger siblings, to a boss or a job, to an idea, to an unfulfilled dream. Not a slavish, demeaning submission to a dubious girl or boy friend or an ungodly philosophy. Is the submission properly directed? Help your daughter grow up and into adulthood with peace and satisfaction and freedom. My son's words are still cheering — "Mom, you were always liberated." Are you? Is she?

No despair in dailiness

September-October 2002

Here I am, chasing cobwebs and wondering just what my niche is. As I tackle the cleaning job, it suddenly strikes me that I am clearing the dust from the fireplace stones that my husband laid there, more than thirty years ago. It doesn't seem as if I am getting ahead. I was enjoying my job until I thought of all this. But maybe I can enjoy it still.

If I count my own years on the job, my children, grandchildren, and great grandchildren, who continue to increase, the number of students that have crossed my path, the pastors and fellow-Christians who have blessed me, the friends and strangers who have come in my front door — and my back — the gardens we have planted, the dishes we have chipped, the knives and forks and spoons that we have lost, the meals that we have cooked and served and eaten, the letters written, the books read, the hymnals worn out, the piano music played to tatters, the sunsets marveled at —I can, at first, feel remarkably set up, and then, humbled, I am put down. I think I feel very much like David in counting his men.

I am helped by the counsel of a seasoned preacher speaking to a group of pastors' wives long ago. His words: "You face the day. You go into the kitchen. Same old dishes to wash. Same old floor to sweep. You pass the day. The door opens. Same old guy to feed." Whatever the nature of our lives, it is the same old something. But how good of the Lord to provide dishes, floors and brooms, a fireplace, to say nothing of the "same old guy."

Every day I see or hear of someone just entering into joys and sorrows that have been mine for years. These are to be welcomed and cherished, not despised. His mercies are new every morning.

Treasures in Jars of Clay

November-December 2002

We have had sickness in the family, and it has been jarring. Why could I not toss it off, ignore it, take it in stride, or exhibit complete confidence in the Lord's knowing what He was doing?

Because I am of little faith, I think. Those days of unseeing eyes and cottony tongue and clawing around for some answer of my own making don't seem so real now, but, for a time, everything else was shut out.

I had been through it before with other family members and, at those times, resolved to steel myself against such suffering again. It didn't work. Clearly, the Lord has suffering in mind for us. He takes us from the valley to the mountaintop and back again. He makes plain His loving-kindness and His severity. He reveals the joy and importance of loved ones and friends. He shows His mighty works in the vulnerability and healing of our bodies. We see our utter weakness before Him and His great mercy toward us.

How could I ignore this fact of sickness when the Lord uses it over and over in the Scriptures to teach us and encourage us? He knows our frame. "Yea, though I walk through the valley of the shadow of death, I will fear no evil, for Thou art with me." (Psalm 23:4)

Jean Belz

Snowfall, right place, right time

January-February 2003

We hadn't had much snow all winter — just an occasional dusting with some wind. Then about two weeks ago it came, a beautiful six-inch layer of pure white snow was spread perfectly over this part of the prairie state. As I walked home in the twilight, I marveled at how the God in heaven had not missed a single twig or corner. The blackish shadows of trees and buildings fell on the purplish cast of the snow in the last minutes of daylight. The white blanket reached in every direction as far as I could see.

But that wasn't enough for everybody. Under severe pressure from hard decisions, careful packing, food preparation, practicing, scheduling, and job after job after job necessary to leave on choir tour only hours later, the men and the students on campus went sledding! Yes, sledding. Weren't they too tired? Of course, there wasn't time. Someone was sure to get hurt. But they went to wonderful Woodpecker Hill in the park some miles away — and were safely back in two hours.

It was as if the snow had sifted out the worries and troubles for everyone — rosy cheeks, friendly smiles, relaxed bodies, willing hearts and kindness all around, and great singing for the "home folks" as the choir warmed up for the first leg of the long trip. The Lord is to be praised for this lovely snowfall at just the right time in just the right place. He is able to do this.

Jean Belz

Our Iowa

May-June 2003

Have you ever driven down an Iowa highway on a June day after a previous day's rain had brought unbelievable freshness? I did that today. As I was pondering the best way to do my errands, I suddenly realized that everything in sight was beautiful. The corn in perfect blue-green rows, the soybeans becoming blankets of lighter green in the fields, the ditches, the swales angling through the fields, white clouds in a blue sky, and even the shoulders of the road trimmed to look like a park — all is lovely. My husband once said that the power mower transformed the countryside. It is true. Do neighbors vie with neighbors for their manicured lawns, flower beds, and plantings of trees and shrubs? If so, I enjoy the contest. Soon the ditches will change color, and the lilies and Queen Anne's lace will take over. A close friend once reminded me, "Never underestimate a lily."

Of course, there is a rugged side. That is, often in a stretch of several miles we see thick groves of trees, impenetrable, it seems. Sometimes a lawn is mowed right up to a piece of rusty machinery. Old buildings still stand here and there. But youngsters from other states often ask, "Where are the trees?" And if you are used to trees growing right down to the side of the road, with no vista, that question is understandable. Our ruggedness is found in the rivers cutting through the hills and bluffs, some running to the southeast into the Mississippi and the others to the southwest to the Missouri. The timber following the riverbeds is beautiful.

Long ago my daughter and her husband moved to a southeastern state. Their neighbor was a teacher and took an intense interest in the geography and history of the state. This rubbed off on my daughter till her interest in her new surroundings affected me. Now that state holds particular interest for me. Learn about where you live and what is special about your state. We are blessed beyond measure.

Jean Belz

Garden variety

July-August 2003

When I read what other people write -- and I am addicted to the printed page — I think, "I should write something profound, something really soulful." But such ideas don't often get down on paper (probably because I am not up to that). Instead some homely, mundane thought keeps interrupting. Now it's the garden!

After years of planting, weeding, and harvesting, a vision of what a vegetable garden actually is popped into my mind -- a plot of ground, large or small, marked off to grow food in an orderly manner. It's not a corn field or a bean field — instead it contains EVERYTHING, and you can always add something else. And there's something for everyone. "Johnny loves green beans." "Bobby won't like the beets." "Auntie loves to can tomatoes." "Don't forget the sugar peas."

And there it is — all that tasty food growing in straight rows or patches. When we dropped the seed into the ground, we expected this to happen. It is amazing. It seems almost presumptuous, but the Lord has assured us, and we are full of faith. Potatoes white with bloom, carrots with their ferny tops, blue-green heads of broccoli, curly parsley in a little short row (this must be right at the kitchen-side of the garden so that you can send even a toddler to pick a few sprigs), ready to add luxury to the dinner table, squash and cucumbers bearing lavishly, big green peppers stuck all the way up the pepper plant — what order and beauty! Neither bugs nor worms, rabbits nor deer pester, and the rain has been plentiful.

As a child I had an idea that the garden stood between us and abject poverty. Maybe it did. I can hear my German father saying to us when we were small, "We go work in the garden." We sighed not knowing the privilege that was ours. Nowadays the garden is a luxury. Every memory is precious, if fleeting, reminding us of earlier strength and vanishing years.

Sister acts

September-October 2003

Is anyone more taken for granted than a sister? You may have cherished or loved a sister and marveled at your close ties. I have enjoyed these ties but without seeing them as a special blessing. I must have thought they were a common thing. Don't lots of people grow up with three sisters?

A few months ago in chatting with a friend about her family, I caught a glimpse of sisters. What a picture of love, understanding, common roots, common goals! I realized I had been neglecting a treasure. Are you saying, "Love?!? You don't know my sister. She's the last person you could love!" Well, give in. Don't tangle. Keep your distance. Pray for her. Consider her lot. Do something so that a mediocre, or worse, relationship becomes more than tolerable, even a joy.

Positively, sisters can delight in each other, not dependent on one another in every decision or having to share in all matters, but enjoying confidence in the other's affairs and praising God together through bane and blessing. I want to say, "We're sisters! We were babies together. We were in the same house. We quarreled, but we understood. We're old now. We don't agree, but we understand."

There are lots of ways to be a sister--by birth, by adoption, in a sisterhood, as a friend, best of all, by being born again in Christ--but today I am rejoicing in the simple meaning it has for women everywhere--my relationship (and mine is happy) to the other women born into my home. Is this your experience? Do you have your sister's cell phone number?

The Franzenburg sisters celebrate their brother Paul's run for Governor of Iowa.

Jean Belz

Finer stuff

November-December 2003

I have become an umbrella woman! I never wanted to be one. I could never keep an umbrella intact--this or that was broken. There was never room for two of us as we walked. It was lost. I forgot it. It was at the other end of the rain shower from me. I couldn't get it up; I couldn't get it down. It seemed like a luxury to me, something I couldn't afford.

But now I have seen the Koreans. They stride across the lawn, up the sidewalk, as if the umbrella is a wrap. (I am more inclined to carry a newspaper over my head.) There are all shapes and sizes. The students can walk along and think or talk about something else. I can't. When I enter the student center, the entrance is filled with all kinds of dripping umbrellas. Beautiful! They give signs of complete confidence on the students' part that they will be there on their return.

If I can learn to carry an umbrella, perhaps I can learn to do some other things--wear a necklace now and then, straighten my collar before I go out, accept a cold drink when all of the time I want a hot one. Stick-in-the-mud, hide-bound, dyed-in-the-wool--none of these terms, in former years, escaped my husband, as he lovingly--I like to think--urged me to try something new. At 84 I really have little hope of change, but I am not turning my back on an umbrella.

Jean Belz

Living Room Donations

January-February 2004

When my grandson gave me a shell he had picked up on a far away beach, he apologized for a broken edge. But I didn't care at all that he couldn't find a perfect one. I loved its beauty and I loved his bringing it all the way home and giving it to me. It is a treasure. So is a lovely copper plate that had to be hammered back into shape following an accident where two other grandsons nearly lost their lives. They were spared, and the not quite smoothed out plate, a gift from one of the boys, is a reminder of God's mercy.

My house looks like a curio shop. It is full of treasures, and they are all gifts. A daughter-in-law could not forget a mug of mine from Jerusalem, broken and glued back together, and she brought a matching tile from the Middle East. Countless gifts from the Czech Republic, India, Ethiopia, Peru, China, and even the United States crowd my shelves and walls, full of meaning and memories. Each one means a special friendship. Which one would I discard?

Family pictures from Germany, pictures recording my childhood to this day–most of a century–and crewel and cross stitch done by daughters and granddaughters are on every side. A "nature" corner holds a piece of bark, a gold finch feather, and a robin's egg shell in a little nest, all offerings of a small grandchild who rushed in breathless with her discoveries.

A faded lilac blossom is only a memory now of a day in May years ago when my young daughter, on a field trip to the state capital building, returned home from the three hour trip barely able to stay awake but determined to give me her gift. She had picked a lilac bloom and kept it, crushed in her hand, all the way home. Its fragrance is still real.

Letters are without price. I have hundreds, but some few are matchless. Nearly thirty years ago, a small granddaughter just learning to write sent this note: "Please let Grandpa see this. And you and him have all my love." That is a treasure unsurpassed.

Jean Belz

The hull in your oats

March-April 2004

Long years ago, more than seventy, I spent the night in the farm home of friends. The man of the house was a huge, jolly-faced man, bald except for the black fringe around his head. He was in charge, but not scary.

At breakfast I approached my bowl of oatmeal cautiously, as was my wont. After all, could I be sure it was pure oatmeal? Suddenly, my host laughed loudly and said, "Ho, ho, ho. I found a hull in my oats!" A hull in his oats!? I never knew if he said it for his own enjoyment or for the benefit of the rest of us, but it changed my life. A hull in his oats! How comforting–reassuring.

How prone I am to fuss about little things–or to bother others with my small worries. Can I learn to shed them or to rise above them? I love to see someone being indifferent to minor troubles or irritations. That person gains stature in everyone's eyes and adds ease to relationships.

Recently, a mother told me that she had just announced, "No whining," to her children when they began to object to a parental decision. Whining comes with small things. If they are big, we can pick up the challenge and battle it out. "No whining" is a good announcement, as is "No quarreling" or "No begging." As we caution our children, are we big enough to see ourselves and to put petty behavior out of our lives? For our leaders down to our youngest children, and for ourselves, we can pray that we will be free of fussing about the "hulls in our oats."

Jean Belz

Wishing for more

May-June 2004

How wonderful that my father and mother should meet in 1914 and marry. She was a young widow with three teenage children, and he was a German immigrant. A turbulent life followed. We five younger children were born. Two great wars were fought with the Great Depression bearing down in between. There were good times and bad times at our house, and we suffered sicknesses and deaths. But for me the air of expectancy was always there, and I had a hope I couldn't explain. It was realized when I put my trust in Jesus Christ.

Ere into being I was brought,
thine eye did see, and in thy thought
my life in all its perfect plan
was ordered ere my days began.

— The Psalter

When my daughter told me a while ago that all her growing up years were wonderful, I could hardly believe it. The oldest of eight, plain surroundings, hard work, limited income, and a small circle of friends! But she said each day had an air of expectancy; she felt privileged. My experience matched hers in many ways.

We hear and see much about the coarsening of our

culture. And I see that our simple way of life balanced with good food, guests, music, reading, flowers, and joy in the world around us gave us a priceless heritage. God is the one who orders this, and He allows parents to deliver it to their children.

Jean Belz

Hangin' in

July-August 2004

What do you do if you persevere? Just wait it out? So often it seems the things we strive for never come about, but enormous blessings come in their place–almost to the point of our forgetting what seemed so important in the first place. Then why bother?

From the vantage point of eighty-five years, it's easier to see everything fall in place. I see younger parents dealing with their children or handling their jobs–sometimes thrashing about and sometimes progressing on an even keel. The years go by, and they are still there. There have been glorious successes and miserable failures along the way. Some have been dealt awful blows; some have struggled with pesky little things. I have seen marriages come to their best years by couples' honoring one another and determining to enjoy those years. And all of these are still on the scene. They have had to face temptation, disillusionment, monotony, sickness and death, loss of income, meanness and insult, even their own failure. And by God's grace, they have overcome. They are still there.

Is it all necessary? Couldn't they just give up? Would anybody care? Don't they deserve to forget the whole thing? Don't some of us have just too many responsibilities? When someone says, "Well, you've done your share," I need to forget that and drive on through. I may have to give up some activity, but I can never go beyond my share of extending prayer, kindness, encouragement, and praise to God. Don't leave the scene. Rejoice in being there.

These are dull, heavy words, but perseverance isn't a light thing. Praise God — it works character, and character, hope.

> *And hope does not disappoint us, because God poured out his love into our hearts by the Holy Spirit, whom he has given us.*
>
> — Romans 5:4

Jean Belz

What shall I then do?

November-December 2004

The question is How To Spend My Time. I probably won't be starting many new projects but I'm ready to enjoy what is going on around me. I love having my boarding boys pass through my dining room, and report on how the day is going. And it is a bright moment when a grandchild pops in.

Reading with the first and second graders isn't just stimulating but a delight. Imagine one of the youngsters interrupting the story out of thin air, to say, "We went fishing last week" or to say, "My uncle died seven years ago" or, sadly, for one budding reader to say, "I think Suzie is mad at me" and the girl in question simply flips her pigtails. We'll never know the depth of Suzie's resentment since we're off to see how the story turns out.

A little girl at church has learned how to read, and when she puts words and notes and volume together the sky is the limit. What joy. Sorrows and pleasures multiply through the years until our sons and daughters, more and more, take on our responsibilities and we suddenly realize that we are the ones being served the coffee or receiving the flowers or being encouraged in our own faith by theirs. Praise be to God.

Love is from God

January-February 2005

Sometimes I cringe a little when someone closes a leave-taking with, "Love ya," — over the phone, in a letter, in a simple parting. What does it mean? Of course, I can't judge the depth of that love. I don't even want to, but it does seem a little freely bestowed.

As a young girl, I dreamed of hearing someone say, "I love you," to me. And in years to follow, someone did, and I know it was a deep love. I know, too, that I didn't appreciate all it meant — a spirit of protection, provision, sacrifice, approval, enjoyment, companionship, but I know now that it was all there.

I remember so clearly hearing a young couple settle a small matter with a few words, and then the relieved young wife said to her husband, "You're so honest," and their eyes and faces exuded understanding and kindness. Is honesty love? Is love honesty?

What do we have for our children? A true love? Do we provide what they need? Sometimes we are fierce about our claims on them, almost prideful. Are we willing to give up some of these claims and supply, instead, the courage it takes to present to them the claims of Christ, to depend on Him in every crisis? This is hard, but surely it is real love.

Not long ago, I heard an elder in the church pray for another elder, a deep-down prayer, and I realized that this was an expression of great love – rooted in the church and powerful, encouraging us all to obedience and confidence. Is this your experience in Christ?

> *Dear friends, let us love one another, for love comes from God.* — 1 John 4:7

Death is the enemy but Jesus is the king

October–December 2005

The cardiologist is comforting and frustrating: "Your general health is good. You look well," followed by a little shake of his head and: "Well, the heart wears out along with the rest of the body." One longs for some kind of signal to gain strength and go back to all the activities of years gone by. No such sign. So this calls for patience and wisdom. And courage. I have heard a number of times that old age is not for sissies. Actually, the doctor, with a few kind words, is capable of extracting warm gratitude from the patient — much like the euphoria that envelops a new mother as she heaps her thanks on the obstetrician. But things are in my favor because the Lord is faithful and good.

We patients are a motley group as we wait our turn. While some are smartly dressed, others are dressed down — even to bib overalls. From necessity or choice? Some have a confident, quick step, and others drag with dim eyes. Kind, cheerful friends or relatives accompany some, but others seem grudging. Even the patients are ungracious at times. Are they so sick, or lacking family or friends, or even simple comforts? Most of the patients are older folks. Have they maintained a sense of humor?

Will they return to a pleasant home? Will loved ones greet them and encourage them?

My favorite story is of an old man who finally reached the end of his patience, rose from his chair, and announced to all those in the waiting room, "Well, I guess I'll just go home and die a natural death." Many of us could turn a little gloom to cheer if we responded as did my friend who told her granddaughter philosophically, "Well, I'm dying, but I'll meet you for lunch." As we anticipate heaven and freedom in Christ from these earthly cares, gratitude and joy give us great peace.

Keep singing

January-March 2006

Recently I listened to an old recording of our school choir. The selections were so choice and the music was so moving and lovely, I had a sort of savage desire to get those students back here just to sing. Why did they go off to careers and marriage and leave us without this pleasure? What were we thinking when they were here? What were they thinking?

We oldsters were concentrating on getting them safely out of the fold, and, no doubt, preparing for the next graduates (who would affect us similarly). The students were champing at the bit, half afraid and half delighted to be on their own.

On this day of nostalgic listening, I wondered why they would want new friends, a job of their very own, or their own home and a spouse and babies. I was much like Mr. Woodhouse in Jane Austen's *Emma* when he was mystified at Emma's governess wanting to go home to her new husband when she could have stayed with the Woodhouses.

But I came to my senses. Years ago when several young single women were feeling restless at the same time that another young mother and I felt burdened with little children, the young mother said kindly, "But you know, they want what we have." Not always, but often true.

Careers are desirable and so are families and children. Great is the woman who takes time for her children and sings too. I read long ago that the famous contralto, Maureen Forrester, added a note to her range at the birth of each of her children — who were several. Who can attain to such heights — and depths? But most mothers can sing a lullaby.

Gardens

April-June 2006

You should see that man's garden! I knew the man as a very small, barefoot boy sitting on the church pew, later performing well in the classroom and on the basketball floor, and I know him now as our athletic director and as a big strapping man of many skills. But I did not expect this garden — with every sort of vegetable — sweet corn soon reaching two feet in height, peas blooming like a picture, tomatoes forming, beautiful hills of squash, and not a weed in sight. He likes it, too, and doesn't share the view of an earlier teacher who grew only vegetables "since you can't eat flowers." This is evidenced by the bright, colorful plantings about his house — although they are mostly the result of his wife's tireless efforts.

A young wife and mother, challenged by her husband to improve her flower beds, has done just that and has lovely borders about her house. Another neighbor struggles valiantly to maintain a rock garden started by a former resident, and she is successful. Her husband sticks to vegetables.

The headmaster's wife, with the help of her menfolk, has changed a rocky barnyard into a beautiful lawn. There are some shrubs transplanted from old, old plantings on campus and others, along with lovely perennials, that were bargains "just waiting to be bought" at the nearby flower shop. At $1.39, they are not to be passed up.

All the gardens are not big. Tiny ones appear under decks and in back yards. One small garden somehow refuses to grow very much, although it boasts a few luscious strawberries. The prize for early, eye-catching color, reminding the rest of us of the great joy of gardening, goes to the business manager and his wife. Besides their own corners of bloom, they faithfully and thoughtfully see that planters are placed here and there, beckoning the visitor to come on in and get acquainted.

When strength is gone, the Lord remembers and provides. That is in contentment just to look and enjoy.

County magistrates

July-September 2006

Q. *What is a trustee?*

A. Someone who has the responsibility of guarding the property or rights of another.

In the present case, he or she is one of a committee of three in the township who are charged with three duties: to be sure all the cemeteries in the township are cared for, to settle fence disputes, and to support the local fire department. His or her name is on the ballot at the regular election, having been secured by ten signatures of citizens of the township. I find this protection of our civil rights remarkable. Does it sound simple to you? It is actually basic to the order of our daily lives here in Iowa.

The county courthouse affects our lives over and over. The assessor decides the amount of property tax we must pay, the treasurer receives that money, the recorder keeps track of land and contracts, boats, snowmobiles, passports, marriage licenses, birth and death certificates, hunting and fishing licenses —among other things. The treasurer's office is where we receive our drivers' licenses — or not. It is a great leveler. I love to sit outside in the parking lot and watch the people come and go — young and old, rich and poor, able and disabled, friendly and self-absorbed, dignified and ill-mannered. I might think I'd get special treatment since I'm old, slow, and surely not impolite. No such thing. The office force seems blind to that.

But now and then their real selves show. When one man, after complaining rather sharply about a certain procedure, asked forgiveness, the lady in charge hugged him as she said, "Young man, anybody can lose his temper, but it takes a man to say he's sorry."

I have read that some folks favor combining various courthouses. The loss of warmth and friendly spirit, even as we settle our differences, would be great. Praise God for the early settlers' wisdom in building a solid foundation of government.

Fitly sungen

January-March 2007

In spite of a terror-stricken world and the effects of sin all about, there is no end of beautiful things we can enjoy. Consider the gray-green shades of swelling buds on the tree branches over on the horizon, the soft sigh of the mourning dove, the smell of damp, raw earth after a shower, the touch of a light breeze on our cheeks, and the taste of spring treats — asparagus, rhubarb. And this is only one season.

But not much matches the written and spoken word. What a gift the Lord has given us! The Scriptures bear me out: "A word aptly spoken is like apples of gold in settings of silver." What a privilege to be able to read and write and speak, and to see the beauty as words are spoken or set down on paper. If, for the first time, we were to come upon even a section of the Psalms or Proverbs or Job or Ruth or similar Bible passages, we would be amazed at their beauty, their loveliness, their poetic insight. Best of all, God makes it clear in John 1:1ff that the Word is God and has saving power.

And here is a glimpse of how some writers have used that Word and more to express praise, wonder, need, humility.

Read Henry Lyte's words: "Praise, my soul, the king

of heaven" — words full of praise that even children love to sing.

The hymnal is full of words taken directly from the Psalms, and the hymns of Isaac Watts make a long list. These hymns are all poems in their own right. Think of "Jesus, my great High Priest, Offered his blood and died."

Sometimes in a worship service my cheeks ache and my eyes well up with tears as I think of the poet's experience in Christ, and I follow his words. What about John Newton's use of "amazing grace" — "twas grace that taught my heart to fear, and grace my fears relieved."

William Cowper's words are full of delight:

"When comforts are declining
He grants the soul again
A season of clear shining
To cheer it after rain."

Does the word *shining* always seem to shine on the page for you? Among Charles Wesley's thousands of lines are these: "Before thy Throne my Surety stands; My name is written on his hands." I hang on tight to *surety* with its promise and simplicity. No need to use big words.

Note the beauty and comfort in George W. Robinson's lines: "I am his, and he is mine." Or in

Philip P. Bliss's: "Once I was blind, but now I can see."

But if all this is too subjective for you, then let your soul rise up with joy, and sing these words of beauty and truth:

Glory be to the Father
And to the Son and to the Holy Ghost;
As it was in the beginning,
Is now and ever shall be
World without end, Amen, Amen.

Jean Belz

60 YEARS AGO

April-June 2007

When we broke custom recently and gathered for our evening service and a picnic around the pond on the farm of a son of the church, I enjoyed — and suffered, too — deep memories as I compared then and now.

Sixty years ago we enjoyed picnics at the farm, too. We called them radish picnics — fried chicken raised and dressed by the housewife, starter yeast rolls with faintly sugary tops, kohlrabi from the garden, sliced cold and crisp, raspberry and ground cherry pie, and then the radishes. With great pleasure, my husband asked our hostess, "How did you think of [the picnic]?" "Well," she said, "I had the radishes."

We still drive over on gravel roads, but I never hear our friends complain of road dust in their houses. Sixty years ago, before our own road was paved, I despaired of keeping our furniture and appliances free of the thick, red dust. Nowadays, homes are closed as air conditioning takes over. There is almost no talk of washing clothes on Monday and ironing on Tuesday or of canning ninety-nine quarts of green beans or of making a dress, but the children still fish and they still take piano lessons.

Would I go back? No, I would not. I enjoyed every one of those days, but I enjoy every one of these. As then, we hope for the same peace and joy of the gospel to be in the heart of each child. As values change worldwide, we know no greater joy than to see the children rest in Christ.

Jean Belz

Still can do

October-December 2007

I love to hear about folks going beyond the ordinary in their later years — we won't all have the stamina, but such stories are a challenge and a joy. I am thinking of the lady nearby, in her nineties, who goes out to civic club meetings nearly every day. But more impressive: she still practices daily on her trumpet and plays Taps on suitable occasion. A long-time friend, in her nineties, has never stopped giving piano lessons to a long list of students.

I marvel at those in their eighties who easily drive their cars here and there. And some sew and some cook.

As for me, I don't "look good." I am like the man who sold his horse with the warning, "He don't look good." The buyer returned the horse, complaining that he was blind, and the original owner replied, "I told you he didn't 'look good.'"

But I want to be put to some use. The fact is there is lots to do. We can't always choose.

I can't fix a whole meal, but I can supply one dish. I can't clean the whole house, but I can sort the magazines and newspapers. I can't do the gardening but I can buy some bulbs. I can't play the accompaniments, but I can encourage the musicians and hear the blue notes.

I can't make all the plans, but I can be cooperative.

I can attend worship services, sing, pray, and listen.

In-laws

April-June 2008

In-laws! Is it a friendly word? As I grew up, it seemed unfriendly. Harsh and not to be desired.

Recently my daughter asked me if I'd ever thought of writing about in-laws. She thinks they are underestimated and neglected. And, in my old age, I do too. I was helped immensely by a friend who always spoke of her husband's parents as "my parents-in-law" with ease and with great respect. Respect is the word — and it soon grows into enjoyment and love.

Well, with eight married children, I am richly blessed with eight children-in-law. A sister once told me that I expected happy relationships, and so they have come about. That may be true. If so, it pays to have great expectations.

But you don't have to have lots of children to enjoy an in-law. We all know single children and their spouses who have loving relationships with parents that convey confidence, trust, pleasure.

I suppose a real test comes when there is criticism, or one offers the other a way to handle a hard problem. Why not take the suggestion, ignore it, or be above it? It's not worth an unhappy disagreement.

Some time after the death of my sister, her much-loved lawyer husband reminded me that he was no longer legally our brother-in-law. But the spirit ruled the law, and he was one of our family. And think of the lasting benefits of family. We share so many interests: gardening, cooking, music, reading, travel, beauty on every side, to say nothing of children of all ages, their careers, their health, their own families. I heard of a man who unfailingly dropped off the mail for his mother-in-law. It is not surprising that this same man's son invited his own mother-in-law to go on a "trip to Bountiful." Kindness is hard to resist.

But you say, "This is all little stuff, and you don't know all my in-law problems." No, I don't, but I know the best thing families can share — the gospel. How wonderfully it unites and gives purpose and understanding. We all want to know what awaits us. It can be nothing but good if we share the truth in Jesus Christ.

Little parades

July-September 2008

When a little eight-year-old girl heard that the annual Fourth of July parade was canceled in our nearby city because of the flood this summer, she got right on top of things. No sulking — just plans. Those plans included a parade in her neighborhood — with dogs and cats, other pets, bicycles and tricycles, scooters and wagons, flyers and music; and candy thrown in by spectators would not be refused. She even hoped for firemen and policemen (who later were reported to have joined the celebration). She thought the parade would last about ten minutes. Can you think of a better way to spend ten minutes? Especially in the midst of discouragement and disappointment — or even devastation?

You may say I am borrowing too much from Pollyanna. I say not so. Parades can come as food, even as a little unhealthy nourishment sometimes. I recall listening long ago to election returns with our candidate losing and our children sunk in despair. In walked Great Grandma with a tray heaped with fresh, homemade sugared doughnuts! The change was electrifying, and not because those gathered were shallow and undiscerning. Sometimes parades are counsel and sometimes example, as in the case of our little organizer.

At almost that same time, July 4, 2008, I read a news

story about the residents of a nearby nursing home. For lack of a parade, they planned their own and marched up and down their hallway. Praise God for those who march, and praise Him for those who want to march.

"A merry heart doeth good like a medicine."

– Proverbs 17:22

Depression Proof

January-March 2009

"Yes, I think I did," I answered after a moment or two of musing over the years. This was in response to a grandchild asking if I lived through the Great Depression. The days are vivid in my mind, so I'm not doubtful concerning the facts. Instead those years pretty much match my entire growing up life. We lived simply and yet with a sense of luxury – that is, holding the food we ate, the music we listened to, and the conversations we held, in high regard. It was a way of life to be held closely in spite of good times or bad times.

When I read of folks who want their lives of affluence restored, who want recovery that will mean an income equal to that of the last twenty or thirty years, I realize they want things that they can touch and see– actually things that fade away.

The twenties, when my father was relatively prosperous, seemed much the same to me as the thirties when he lost everything he owned. We never expected easy times. I know now that my father agonized over our plight, and my mother suffered. I recall a Christmas eve when a kind neighbor, the druggist's wife, gave mother a bottle of skin crème with the tag reading, "Now indulge in a bit of luxury." What wonder! Any such gift was prized.

College was not taken for granted either. Some had to wait or not go at all. Courses were removed from secondary schools. Somehow the lacks were not seen as disastrous. We enjoyed our meals, and our made-over clothing did not prevent friendships or marriages. We could still sing and learn to play the piano and other instruments. We could read, debate, and enjoy our own drama. And we could go to church. Even today, in the midst of the financial change, I read headlines predicting a drop in giving and supporting the Lord's work. But in our little circle, we see it continuing and even increasing. No matter the times, "where your treasure is, there will your heart be also." —Matthew 6:21

It takes a (caring) village

January-March 2010

When the time came to decide where I should be in my declining years, all my children — and there are many — were very kind. I was on the verge of packing up when we realized a move might not be necessary after all. Other folks have stayed in their houses and I am blessed with help on every side in the Cono community. The people of the church and school rose to the occasion to help me at 90 years of age.

Some folks wouldn't care for the advantages I have had. I love having a guest room that is nearly always available to parents of students, visitors, family. If I don't make it so, I miss out on making a host of friends. Little girls come with the first blooms of spring — on sale for just a few cents. Little boys come looking for a job expecting only a small wage. Students come for an interview concerning my life on campus. Neighbors come in for cookies and coffee. A grandson comes home from work, weary but cheerful. A granddaughter plays all her piano contest selections. A neighbor boy fills my wood box. What treats! The mail comes. There's a fresh e-mail. On a mild day, I can walk to church.

A tasty supper comes in from the school kitchen, graciously delivered, no grudging. And there are no complaints about the weather. Nothing is better than a crowd barging in armed with hymn books and spending an hour in a capella singing — unless it's a special group of boys or girls practicing their latest choir song. A son and his wife look after business affairs and errands — cheerfully, lovingly.

I can still direct the affairs of my house so I am glad to be here. When I can't, may I praise God for keeping me in His own way. He is faithful.

Teen Publishing

April-June 2010

It took a friend's attention to remind me of the value of saving certain relics of the past. I'll admit to losing some interest in examining many papers and pictures as the years go by and laying them aside. We were sorting such things when my helper said, "What's this?"

Rather indifferently I said, "My high school newspaper."

With much urging and interest on her part, we dug up bits of information from the 1930s. While I sorted other items, she read aloud from the paper — I had won a watch! I had won two watches! There were veiled references to certain friendships, all important in May 1936, and soon forgotten when "real" life set in. There were columns full of class news, alumni news, music, and sports. The pages were well balanced.

Now it came back to me — learning to gather the news, persuading the students to get their news in, dealing with an unreliable printer, being blessed by a faithful friend who worked into the wee hours to help meet a deadline. It was drudgery and exhilarating at the same time.

My mother had suggested THE TATLER as the name of our student newspaper. Whether or not the original editors, in the 17th century, Joseph Addison and Richard Steele, used a double *t* or a single *t* is unimportant.

I married a man who loved the printed page and now our grandchildren cannot resist writing their own blogs.

Best of all, we have God's word and it is written!

Trees, changing, established

July-September 2010

The tree men came. There was a little anxiety on the part of some before they arrived. Some of the old maples looked ready to fall in a bad wind storm or even with no storm at all.

The men had heavy machinery and lots of skills. Several trees were soon on the ground and many others were trimmed. My impulse was to run out and say, "no, not that one." It had always been that way. Each one has significance to me — the apple tree that seeded itself and then bore wonderful apples. The birch trees that school boys and I dug up at the river. They are so tough and their multiple trunks make a most desirable tree. Mr. Al Ferguson, then our local nursery man, planted two sunburst locusts years ago even though he said "they aren't much of a tree." Most of the arbor vitae behind Alling Hall are gone. The red buds and flowering crabs are holding their own, and a beautiful variegated lilac escaped the woodman's axe. Not so with the row of poplars that marked the west side of the soccer field. Wind and decay brought on their demise, but a fine windbreak has taken their place to complete the rows of evergreens edging the entire property on the west. We are assured that in no time at all this wind break will hold back tons of snow besides furnishing all a photographer might desire for a subject.

Besides all this, younger trees and shrubs are taking hold and a huge magnolia and several sturdy hard maples are lovely. The 2010 graduating class set out two maples and two apple trees — a wonderful gift. The campus is not treeless, but shady and cool. It invites you to come. The Lord teaches us to wait and take what comes from His hand. He is faithful and good.

Jean Belz was able to attend Hamline University in St. Paul for one year during the Depression, then married, and with her husband Max, founded Cono Christian School in 1951. She taught English literature and Latin to teenagers for more than 50 years.

She would have been 92 in May 2011.

Available at amazon.com
under this title and author

36552552R00136

Made in the USA
Lexington, KY
24 October 2014